A SURVEY OF
WORLD CULTURES

AFRICA

Ken Levine

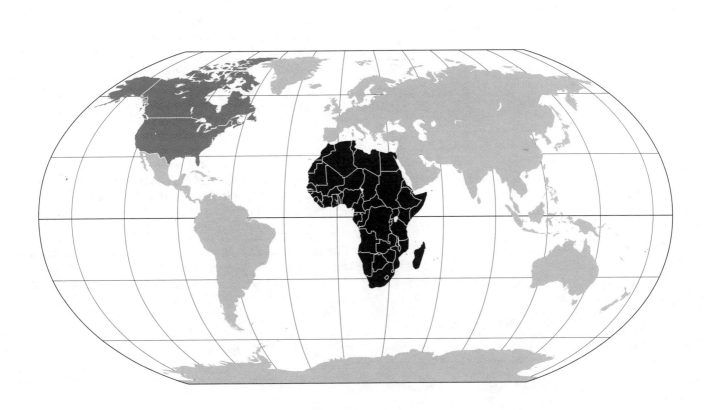

AGS®

A SURVEY OF WORLD CULTURES

AFRICA

Ken Levine

Ken Levine published numerous non-fiction articles before writing this book. In addition, he teaches on the secondary level in Baltimore County, Maryland.

Photo Acknowledgements

Cover Photographs: Upper left: Jonathan Blair/Corbis; upper right: Wendy Sjoblom; lower left Farmar/Leo de Wys, Inc., Wide World Photos

Chapter 1: Page 2, James Kennedy from *Europus Kolonien*; page 5, Judy King; page 11, courtesy of National Geographic; page 13, SuperStock; Page 18, Frank Wood/SuperStock

Chapter 2: page 23 B. Press, Woodfin Camp & Associates, Inc.; page 24, Kimbell Art Museum/Corbis; page 29, Library of Congress; Page 32, K. Muller, Woodfin Camp & Associates, Inc.

Chapter 3: Page 42, W. Robert Moore/NGS Image Collection; page 45, B. Press, Woodfin Camp & Associates, Inc.; page 46, Charles O'Rear/Corbis

Chapter 4: Page 50, Christine Osborne/Corbis; page 53, SuperStock; page 54, Kevin Fleming/Corbis; page 57, B. Press, Woodfin Camp & Associates, Inc.; Page 60, Holton Collection/SuperStock

Chapter 5: Corbis; page 69, AFP/Corbis; page 82, Guy Stubbs; Gallo Images/Corbis; page 72, United Nations; page 75, United Nations; page 77, Charles & Josette Lenars/Corbis; page 81, Adrian Arbib, Corbis; Page 84, SuperStock

Chapter 6: Pages 90, 91, Library of Congress; page 107, The Illustrated London News; page 96, James Blair/NGS Image Collection; page 99, United Nations photo/AID/Purcell; pages 102, 105, Judy King; page 97, Dennis Degnan, Corbis; Page 108 Michele Burgess/ SuperStock

Chapter 7: Page 113, Kenneth Garrett/NGS Image Collection; page 115, Thomas Abercrombie/NGS Image Collection; page 116, Dennis Marsico/Corbis; page 117, B. Iverson, Woodfin Camp & Associates, Inc.; page119, Tiziana and Gianni Baldizzone/Corbis; page 123, Ray Manley/ SuperStock

ISBN: 0-7854-2627-2

Product No. 90932

A 0 9 8 7 6 5 4 3 2

CONTENTS

CONTENTS

CONTENTS

AFRICA
INTRODUCTION

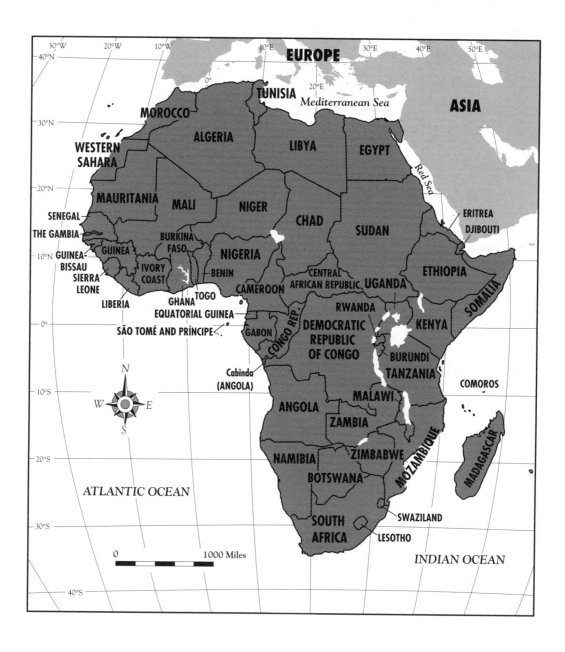

What Is Culture?

People all over the world have the same basic needs. But they meet these needs in different ways. They learn their ways of thinking and acting—**traditions**—from their ancestors. These traditions are known as culture.

Culture is the way people live. Culture is what people believe. It is how a group of people behaves with one another, and how they behave with people outside their group. Culture is what makes every group of people special and unique.

Culture is made up of many different things. Culture is the language, music, and art of a people, and the holidays they celebrate. It is their **economic** system and the ways they are governed. It is the ways they dress and the products they produce. It is the customs, religions, and inventions that a group of people shares.

Humans have lived on Earth for a very long time. During this time, the ways people live have changed. Humans have learned to adapt and use their environment to survive. The climate and the kinds of food that were available have given people certain choices. They have figured out what to use for clothing and shelter to keep themselves warm and dry, and what to eat to make themselves strong and healthy. Most important, humans have learned to communicate. This process of adapting to the environment and learning how to communicate marked the beginning of culture.

Why We Need to Understand Culture

Understanding a nation's culture isn't easy. But we need to know something about cultures around the world for at least three reasons.

First, studying culture helps us to understand ourselves better. Studying culture helps us to understand why we act and live the ways we do.

Second, understanding culture helps us to more effectively deal with change. We understand things like how people might feel about new inventions and discoveries that will affect their lives.

Third, understanding culture helps us to work better with people of other nations and cultures. We understand that we may see things very differently from each other. Knowing this helps us to work together for a better future.

Exploring Culture in This Book

Africa is a land of great **potential**. Millions of Africans are just now emerging onto the world stage. Exciting growth is being made in a continent that has, for centuries, been underdeveloped.

INTRODUCTION

Words to Know

developing country:
a country improving in technology and quality of living after becoming self-governing

economic:
having to do with earning a living and producing goods and services

ethnic:
a group of people who share a common culture and history

potential:
possibility of future development and improvement

rain forest:
a thick tropical forest

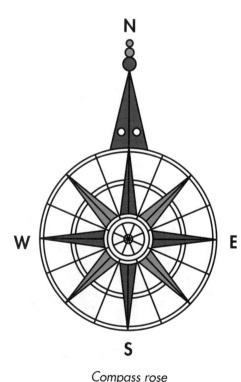

N

W   E

S

Compass rose

But Africa is also a land with many problems. **Ethnic** warfare, AIDs, drought, and famine continue to cause terrible suffering throughout Africa.

Today, we are in the position of knowing quite a lot about Africa—and, at the same time, not knowing enough. Our newspapers are full of the daily events that occur on the continent of Africa. What we sometimes lack is the overall picture into which each of these news events may be fitted.

This book is designed to give you a full picture of modern Africa. Africa is the second largest continent in the world. All of the land of the United States could fit within its borders. Africa is bordered on the west by the Atlantic Ocean and on the east by the Indian Ocean. To the north and the northeast are the Mediterranean Sea, the Suez Canal, and the Red Sea. The Cape of Good Hope lies at this continent's southernmost tip.

In Africa you will find steaming **rain forests**, dry deserts, mountain peaks, endless grasslands, and miles of beautiful coastline. The human population and culture are as varied as the geography. In fact, in Africa there are more than 2,000 different ethnic groups and over 800 languages spoken!

In this book, you will be looking at the cultural patterns developed by the people of Africa. You will be introduced to the geography of the various regions of Africa and see how this setting has affected the history, economics, and culture of the African people. The book explores some of the successes, problems, and prospects for the future of the **developing countries** of Africa.

Remember that the real story of Africa is its people, just as the story of the United States or of any other nation is mostly a story of its people.

Learning about Maps and Globes

You need to know the meaning of some terms to understand maps. A *map* is a picture of the earth, or part of the earth, on a flat piece of paper. A *sphere* is a round body, or a ball. A *globe* is a round ball that stands for the earth. A *hemisphere* is half of this globe.

Maps and globes can show different things. There are many different kinds of maps. For example, a *physical map* shows such things as mountains, rivers, and plains. A *political map* shows borders between states or countries. A *climate map* shows hot, cold, dry, and wet areas. A *natural resources* map shows things like the locations of minerals and oil. Maps and globes can also help you understand the relationships among these things. All of these things influence culture.

The *equator* is an imaginary line around the middle of the earth. It separates the earth into the *Northern Hemisphere* (above the equator) and the *Southern Hemisphere* (below the equator).

INTRODUCTION

A *legend* on a map will explain the meaning of any symbols on the map. It may also have a measure that is equal to a certain number of miles. That way, you can find out how far apart the locations on a map really are.

Lines of *latitude* are imaginary lines running east and west (across) on a map. These lines measure, by degrees, the distance north or south of the equator. A *degree* is a unit of measure. The equator is zero degrees. One degree of latitude is approximately 69 miles. So, places along the 10 degrees north parallel line are 690 miles from the equator. Latitude lines are sometimes called *parallels* because they are the same distance apart from each other, no matter where they are located.

Lines of *longitude* are also imaginary lines drawn on a map. They run north and south (up and down). They measure the distance east or west of the *prime meridian* (see below). These lines of longitude, called *meridians*, are the same distance apart at the equator. However, they are not parallels because they do not stay the same distance apart. If you move from the equator to the North Pole or the South Pole, the distance around the globe gets smaller. The distance between lines of longitude decreases as you move away from the equator. All of the lines of longitude come together at each of the poles.

The *prime meridian* is a line that runs around the world from the North Pole to the South Pole. It goes through Greenwich, England. It is located at the zero degree meridian. It separates the earth into the Eastern Hemisphere and the Western Hemisphere.

A *compass rose* like the one shown here can be found on many maps. It shows which way north is located and may show other major directions as well. Remember that north is a direction. Usually, but not always, it is placed at the top of a page.

In this book, you will see a small map in the lower right-hand corner of every right-hand page. This map shows the whole continent of Africa. As you move through the book, the country you're studying will appear black on that map.

Each chapter in this book begins with a Map Skills exercise. This exercise will introduce you to the country you will study in the chapter. It will also give you a chance to become more familiar with the terms you've read about in this introduction.

Studying the maps in this book will help you to learn about the cultures of Africa.

REVIEW

Answer the following questions.

1. What is the difference between a globe and a map?
2. What is the equator? How does it divide the globe?
3. What is the prime meridian? How does it divide the globe?
4. In what direction do latitude lines run?
5. How do latitude lines measure distance from the equator?
6. In what direction do longitude lines run?
7. How do longitude lines measure distance from the prime meridian?
8. What is a hemisphere?

COASTAL WEST AFRICA
CHAPTER 1

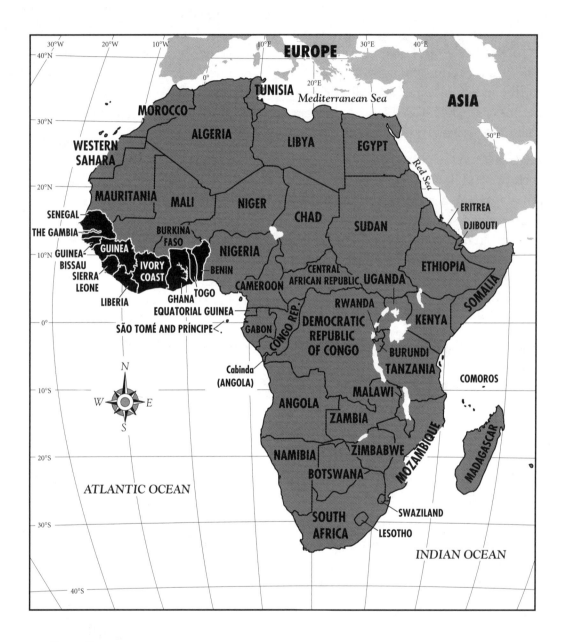

Fast Facts:

- More than 500 African ethnic groups live in West Africa.
- The basic unit of money in Senegal is the franc.
- Liberia and Sierra Leone were set up as countries where freed slaves could live.
- Independence Day in Gambia is celebrated on February 18.
- Drums are an important part of life in Ghana.

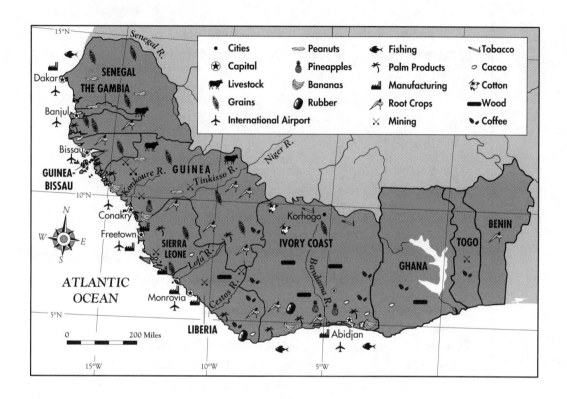

MAP SKILLS

Products of Coastal West Africa

Study the map above to answer these questions.

1. What trees are grown near the mouth of the Cestos River in Liberia?

2. What two crops are grown near Korhogo in the Ivory Coast?

3. Name three cities in which one might find an international airport.

4. Which of these is not to be found near Freetown in Sierra Leone: palm products, mining, fishing, or manufacturing?

5. Name three products found near the Tinkisso River in Guinea.

6. Name two countries in which peanuts are grown.

Words to Know

cash crop:
a crop that is raised for sale and export rather than for one's own use

Christianity:
the religion derived from Jesus Christ and based on the Old Testament and New Testament of the Bible as sacred scripture

coastal plain:
a flat, sea-level area usually near an ocean

economy:
the way in which a group or nation provides for the needs and desires of its people

Islam:
a world religion stating the belief that Allah is the only god and the Muhammad is his prophet

millet:
any of several cereal grasses, grown for food or hay

Muslim:
a person who follows the religion of Islam

phosphate:
a salt of phosphoric acid used in bread or fertilizer

savanna:
a tropical grassland with scattered trees

sorghum:
grain used for food, roofs, and to feed animals

LESSON 1: Atlantic Coast Countries

West Africa is one of the most densely settled parts of Africa. The people have settled mainly on the **coastal plain** and on the dry **savanna** region along the southern edge of the Sahara. This area is called the Sahel.

Today, there are more than 500 African ethnic groups living in West Africa. Bantu-speaking people make up the largest ethnic groups. They live in the forest regions near the coast.

These coastal people were the first to come into contact with the Europeans. They were also the first to suffer from the effects of the slave trade. **Christianity** was introduced to the coastal peoples by European missionaries.

The people of the much drier Sahel region have had a long history of contact with the **Islamic** civilization. These **Muslims** live across the Sahara Desert in North Africa.

Despite extreme cultural pressure from Muslims, who follow the Islamic religion, and Christians, many traditional beliefs in nature and in spiritual beings have continued. Both Islamic and Christian ideas have been adapted to the traditional West African culture.

Coastal West Africa consists of ten different countries. These countries can be divided into two different regions: the Atlantic Coast countries and the Guinea Coast countries.

The Wolof make up more than one-third of the population of Senegal and The Gambia.

2

Senegal and The Gambia

Senegal is located at the western extreme of Coastal West Africa. Almost all of the land of Senegal lies in the Sahel, a flat dry savanna, or grassland. Senegal surrounds the nation of The Gambia.

The people of Senegal and The Gambia consist mainly of five ethnic groups. The largest, called the Wolof, make up more than one-third of the population. The other ethnic groups include the Serer, the Dioula, and the Malinke or Mandingo. Islam is the religion of most of the people. Traditional culture is still strong.

The people of the region have adapted much from the outside. Gambians speak English as well as their traditional languages. Senegal was the center of the French empire in West Africa. Dakar, its capital, was the main city of the region. French is the official language of Senegal, but local traditional languages are also very important.

Most of the people of Senegal and The Gambia make a living through farming on the savanna. Peanuts, called groundnuts in West Africa, are often grown in irrigated fields. They are the main **cash crop** for export. **Millet** and **sorghum,** corn, and rice are also grown. In addition to these crops, farmers raise cattle, chickens, sheep, and goats. Gambians depend on the Gambia River as a water supply for farming.

In recent years, Senegal's **economy** has improved. Dakar has factories that process cotton, rice, and **phosphate** ore. Construction, electronics, and government services are important activities that create jobs.

Many women of Senegal have become active in the work force. A number of women are successful owners and managers of retail businesses. Some women have moved into other professions, particularly nursing and teaching, but also medicine and law.

Since the prosperity of the two countries depends on one crop, the nation's economy rises and falls with the price of peanuts.

History of Senegal and The Gambia

Senegal and The Gambia have a long and colorful history. That history is told orally by a *griot*, a traditional historian who recites poems telling of the deeds of the past. The griots have formed a long unbroken chain of history in an area of the world where history books were written only in Arabic. Traditional customs and beliefs are passed down from generation to generation in the form of stories. Being a griot in Senegal is much like being a history teacher or a historian in the United States.

Words to Know

bauxite:
a mineral ore used in making aluminum

cassava:
a tropical plant with starchy roots; tapioca is made from cassava root

colony:
a group of people living in a territory but keeping ties with the parent nation

palm:
tall trees with tall trunk and branches, with large leaves at the top; palm kernals are used to make food oil and starch, and palm fiber is used to make rope

topography:
the surface features of the land

The Gambia River has always played a major role in the history of The Gambia. Beginning in the 1500s, slaves were traded along its banks. One village on the banks of this river is the city of Jufureh. Writer Alex Haley traced his ancestors to this city and wrote the story of the origin of his own Mandingo family. Perhaps you have seen the movie *Roots*, which is based on Haley's book of the same name.

LESSON REVIEW

Directions: Number your paper from 1 to 6. Write True or False for each statement.

1. Most farming in Senegal is done on the savanna.
2. Peanuts are exported by both Senegal and The Gambia.
3. In addition to traditional languages, English is spoken in The Gambia and French in Senegal.
4. Senegal has the most developed economy of the Atlantic Coast countries.
5. The griots of Senegal are much like history teachers in America.
6. Alex Haley, in his novel *Roots*, traced his ancestors to a region of Sierra Leone.

LESSON 2: Guinea and Guinea-Bissau

Southeast of Senegal and Gambia is the Republic of Guinea. Its **topography** is that of a plain broken by rolling hills. This plain is covered by tall-tree savannas and dry forests. Guinea has both fertile farmland and valuable mineral resources. Cash crops include coffee, bananas, peanuts, and palm products from oil palm trees. This oil is used to make cosmetics, soap, and cooking oils.

Palm kernels are used to make food and starch, while the palm fiber is used to make mats and rope. **Cassava** is the main food crop raised. Rice, corn, bananas, and pineapples are also raised for food. Guinea produces one-third of the world's **bauxite**, a valuable mineral ore used to make aluminum. In addition, Guinea has large deposits of iron ore as well as gold and diamond mines.

Cassava is the main food crop raised in Guinea.

Guinea has a proud historical tradition. During the 700s, Guinea was a major trading kingdom called Guinea. Later, the country became a possession of France. After long years as a French **colony**, the people of Guinea voted in 1958 to become independent under the leadership of Sekou Toure.

Three major ethnic groups live in Guinea. The largest is the Peul. Next in size are the Malinke and the Sossou. Within the forests of Guinea also live the Kissi, the Guerze, and the Loma. Most of the people of Guinea, regardless of their particular ethnic background, live in small villages. The official language of the country is French.

Words to Know

cacao:
the seeds from which cocoa and chocolate are made

piassava:
a palm tree whose fibers are used to make brooms

subsistence:
producing a minimum return and a level of bare existence

Guinea-Bissau: A Tropical Land

Guinea-Bissau used to be known as Portuguese Guinea. It is one of the smallest countries in Africa. The capital city of Guinea-Bissau is Bissau. It is the biggest city in this tiny country. The city was an important port during the Portuguese slave trade. The official language of the country is Portuguese.

This country's land is flat and has many rivers. Guinea-Bissau's climate is typical of a tropical country. It has a dry season during which there is little or no rain. This season lasts from December to May. The rainy season lasts from June to November, with the heaviest rains coming in July and August.

Living Conditions

Ninety percent of the people in Guinea-Bissau earn their living from farming. Many different kinds of crops are grown. Farmers grow rice, cassava, palm kernels, corn, peanuts, and cotton. The farmers of Guinea-Bissau are mainly **subsistence** farmers. That term means that they usually grow food only for their own families rather than for sale. However, peanuts and palm kernels are export crops.

Most of the people of Guinea-Bissau live in small villages throughout the country. The houses are very similar to those in neighboring countries—usually made of mud and straw with a thatched roof.

Many different ethnic groups can be found in Guinea-Bissau. The largest of these groups are the Balante, the Fului, the Manjako, and the Mandingo. There are perhaps 20 ethnic groups living in Guinea-Bissau.

LESSON REVIEW

Directions: Number your paper from 1 to 4. Then answer the following questions.

1. What is the capital city of Guinea-Bissau?

2. What products make the land in Guinea valuable?

3. What Guinean crop has a root that can be eaten?

4. Why do you think that Guinea-Bissau was once known as Portuguese Guinea?

LESSON 3: Sierra Leone and Liberia

Continuing south along the coast of West Africa, we come to Sierra Leone. A very large portion of the population here are farmers. Most of Sierra Leone's farmers grow rice and cassava as their main food crops. Some farmers also grow a type of palm tree that produces **piassava**, a product exported to make brooms and brushes. Other cash (export) crops are coffee and **cacao**, which is used in making chocolate.

Textile Dyeing and Other Industries

A traditional art, textile dyeing, has developed into an important industry in Sierra Leone. Originally, dyes made from vegetables were used. Today, commercial dyes are used to produce the finished goods.

Many times a successful dyer will employ family members to produce the colorful cloth. Textile dyers earn a good income. Other industries are centered around food processing and building supplies.

Diamonds Are an Important Export

The people of Sierra Leone have one other product to export—diamonds. These stones are mined from gravel beds as little as four feet deep. Many of the diamonds are used for industrial purposes. However, many stones are also cut and polished and sold as gems. Unfortunately, money from the sale of smuggled diamonds has often gone to help rebel soldiers. These rebels have killed or injured tens of thousands of civilians. The governments of Sierra Leone and other countries took steps in late 2000 to stop the smuggling of diamonds.

Living in Sierra Leone

The capital city of Sierra Leone is Freetown. This city has many modern buildings and a large open air market. In contrast, houses in villages are usually made from mud and have thatched roofs.

The Ethnic Groups of Sierra Leone

The people of Sierra Leone come chiefly from two ethnic groups. The Mende live in the south of the country, and the Temne live in the west. Many descendants of mixed races also live throughout the country. These people are called Creoles and they speak Krio, a form of English. Their ancestors came mostly from freed slaves and whites from England and Canada. The official language of Sierra Leone is English.

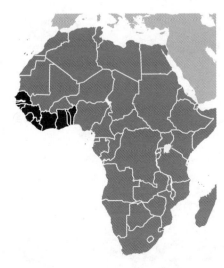

Words to Know

mangrove:
tropical trees or shrubs with many roots that look like extra trunks and form dense masses

synthetic:
not real; artificial

Liberia

Liberia is located on the bulge of West Africa. It is bounded by Sierra Leone, Guinea, and the Ivory Coast. Its coastal plain touches both the Atlantic Ocean and the Gulf of Guinea.

Along the coast are **mangrove** swamps. Most of the inland area is plains covered with tall-tree savannas and tropical rain forests. Farther inland is an area of low mountains covered with thick, wet tropical forests.

Most Liberians practice subsistence farming. Cassava and rice are the main food crops. Coffee, cacao, and palm products are the main export crops. Rubber plantations owned by the American Firestone Rubber Company once controlled the Liberian economy. However, with the development of **synthetic** rubber, this product is not quite as important as it once was to the economy.

Today, the mining of large deposits of high grade iron ore has helped the economy of Liberia. Bauxite, used to make aluminum, is mined both in Liberia and Sierra Leone.

Settlements for Freed Slaves

Both Liberia and Sierra Leone were founded as settlements for freed slaves. Liberia was founded in 1822 by freed slaves from the United States. The name Liberia comes from the Latin word *liber*, which means "free." About five percent of the almost three million Liberians can trace their descent from freed slaves.

The country became a republic in 1847, with a constitution and government modeled after those of the United States. The Liberians speak English, practice Christianity, and follow Western styles of social organization.

Beginning in 1787, the British Society for the Abolition of Slavery purchased land from the Temne people. Slaves who were freed or who had escaped from the United States or the West Indies were welcomed to this land. Thousands of slaves who had been freed from slave ships by the British navy were also settled there. The region would become known as Sierra Leone.

In the 1800s, Sierra Leone became a British colony. In 1961, it gained its independence and became a republic.

LESSON REVIEW

Directions: Number your paper from 1 to 6. Write the name of the ethnic group or nation described by each statement.

1. This group lives in the southern part of Sierra Leone.

2. These descendants of freed slaves share Sierra Leone with the Mende and Temne ethnic groups.

3. This nation was founded by slaves freed by the British.

4. This nation was founded by freed slaves from the United States.

5. Rubber exports once made up the most important part of this nation's economy.

6. Once a British colony, this nation became independent in 1961.

Words to Know

animism:
the belief that spirits occupy all objects, both living and nonliving

hardwood:
a tree that does not produce its seeds in cones

LESSON 4: Guinea Coast Countries—Ivory Coast, Ghana, Togo, and Benin

Once the country called the Ivory Coast was a place where many, many elephants could be found. The tusks of elephants are made of ivory, a product greatly treasured in Europe and the United States. Now most of the elephants are gone. During the colonial era, they were killed by the thousands for their tusks—some of which weighed up to 200 pounds each. However, the people of the Ivory Coast, called Ivorians, have many other resources to rely upon. Rich fertile soil and plenty of water make the Ivory Coast one of the most productive nations of the world. In fact, it has one of the most developed economies in Africa.

The Ivory Coast is located on the Gulf of Guinea. The official name is Republic of Côte d' Ivoire. This country is bounded by Liberia, Guinea, Mali, Burkina Faso, and Ghana. The coastline extends for 315 miles, and neither bay nor cape breaks its regular shape. The coastal plain extends inland for about 40 miles. Beyond the coastal plain the land rises to a plateau with an elevation of more than 1,000 feet.

The climate near the coast is always warm and wet. The two rainy seasons are separated by less humid periods. In these coastal areas, the heat and rainfall create a tropical rain forest. On the plateaus, temperatures are lower due to the higher altitude, and there is a dry season. In the plateau region there is a grass savanna.

The Ivory Coast chose to concentrate first on developing the agricultural segment before encouraging industry. This country is developing a strong market for its tropical agriculture products. It has made great efforts to increase such crops as pineapples, bananas, and sugar. Coffee and cacao production has been expanded. The Ivory Coast leads the world in the production of cacao and is third in coffee production.

Of course, the Ivorians still grow other typical African crops like millet, rice, peanuts, and cassava. Another major crop in the Ivory Coast is timber. The Ivorian government treats timber as a crop. They plant and harvest trees just as many responsible tree-growers in America do: to protect the forest's future. The Ivory Coast leads Africa in the production of tropical **hardwoods**.

Oil—A New Industry

The Ivory Coast receives large amounts of money from foreign investors. As a result, the Ivory Coast has begun to produce oil. Enough oil comes from its off-shore wells to supply most of the country's needs.

Rush hour traffic in Abidjan, the capital of the Ivory Coast.

Manufacturing strengthens the Ivory Coast's already strong economy. Goods manufactured include chemicals, aluminum, and automobiles.

The capital city of the Ivory Coast is Abidjan. This modern capital is a major port and also the location of many industries. Two other important cities are Bouaké and Yamoussoukro. Most of the approximately 15 million people in the Ivory Coast live either in small villages or in the country. French is the official language, because the Ivory Coast was once a French colony. However, over 60 different languages are spoken.

Religions and Traditional Practices

Many ethnic groups live in this country, including the Beti, Senufo, and the Anvi, plus a dozen other ethnic groups. About 60 percent of the people are Muslims, 25 percent native religions, and about 12 percent are Christian. The Muslim religion forbids the eating of pork, so people in this part of the world do not raise pigs.

Ethnic religions are based on **animism**, the belief that spirits occupy all objects, both living and nonliving. Some of these spirits are helpful, while others are harmful. In traditional society, a priest or chief keeps his people living peacefully with a combination of law, ritual, and magic.

Words to Know

civilian:
a person who is not in the armed services or military

coup d'etat:
attempt made by the military to overthrow a government

javelin:
a light spear thrown by hand

sub-Saharan:
Africa south of the Sahara

A Strong and Stable Government

The Ivory Coast had a very stable government for more than 50 years. The president during most of that time was a man named Felix Houphouet-Boigny. It is Houphouet-Boigny who gets the credit for taking the Ivory Coast from a colony to a well-run, independent country. Today the president of the country is Henri Konan Bedie.

The southern part of the Ivory Coast provides the best health conditions and services. Educational and job opportunities are also very good here. Many subsistence farmers are leaving the dry north to seek jobs in the cities and towns of the south.

Ghana's Past Glory

Possibly the earliest kingdom in **sub-Saharan** Africa was the Empire of Ghana. This empire was at its greatest height from the fourth to the eleventh century. It spread from the Atlantic Ocean to the Niger River and from the Sahara Desert south to below the Niger River. The capital city of Koumbi was described by an eleventh century Arab historian, El Bakri. Koumbi had as many as 15,000 people living within its walls. Archaeologists have uncovered evidence of a great civilization. The windows of the king's home were made of glass, a product that had not yet come into Europe at that time.

The Ghanaians boasted, with good reason, that their university at Timbuktu was the oldest center of advanced learning in the world. (Timbuktu is now located in Mali.) Scholars from all parts of the world came there to study.

Although most of the people of the Empire of Ghana were farmers, the power and wealth of Ghana depended on three resources—gold, salt, and iron. The Ghana, or ruler, controlled all the gold in the empire. Gold was so important that the word *ghana* itself came to mean "gold." Salt was also vital to all the nations of the area. In fact, gold and salt were once given equal value. Iron was the vital metal used to produce weapons—spears, **javelins**, and swords. Ghana depended on the trans-Sahara trade in gold, salt, and iron for its very existence.

Modern Ghana

Ghana became an independent nation in 1957. This area was the first British colony in sub-Sahara Africa to gain independence.

The first elected leader to be head of the Ghana government was Kwame Nkrumah. He was a school teacher who had been educated in the United States. Upon his return to Ghana after his studies, he established a political party called the Convention People's Party.

Nkrumah proved to be a strong leader. He was an excellent politician and public speaker and gained the respect of all the people of his country. As a result of his enthusiasm, the people were willing to work very hard to achieve independence.

However, things quickly changed once Nkrumah became president. He made many policy changes. He increased his personal power and imprisoned some people who criticized the government. People began to fear the government. Many people felt that unwise decisions had damaged the economy and left the country with many large debts.

This government was overthrown in 1966, while Nkrumah was in China. A new National Liberation Council, headed by General Joseph Ankrah, ruled the country. Under this leadership, the country was returned to civilian rule.

Since that time, Ghana's political system has been unstable. The country has experienced **coups d'etat** and has switched back and forth several times between **civilian** and military rule. Perhaps the best-known person from Ghana is Kofi Annan, who in 1997 became secretary general (the highest office) of the United Nations.

Modern Ghana's Economy

Cacao continues to be an important cash-export crop for Ghana. However, due to the fall in world prices and to a government policy that neglected replanting, many farmers lost money and became discouraged.

As a result, many Africans who had worked on the cacao plantations returned to their homes and traditional ways. Subsistence farming has increased greatly over the past 30 years. Ghana's farmers raise cassava, millet, sorghum, yams (sweet potatoes), and corn.

The people of Ghana are famous for their woodcarvings.

Words to Know

manganese:
hard, brittle, grayish metallic element used to make steel, in paints, dyes, etc.

preserve:
a place where wild animals roam freely and are protected by law from hunters

protectorate:
a weak country under the protection and partial control of a strong country

Dependence on one crop—cacao—has presented many problems. Attempts to set up other industries have been partly successful. A hydroelectric plant on the Volta River produces great amounts of electric power. A large aluminum plant, a steel mill, and an oil refinery have been built. Minerals such as bauxite for aluminum and **manganese**, used in making steel, as well as gold and diamonds, are being mined. Ghanaians are famous for their woodcarvings, and woodworkers are valued.

Approximately 30 percent of Ghana's population lives in cities. The capital city of Ghana is Accra. This large, modern city has many shops, office buildings, restaurants, and banks. Most people get around Accra by walking or taking buses and taxis. Only a small percentage of the people owns cars.

Although there are dozens of different ethnic groups in Ghana, most of the people are from a large group called the Akan. Most people speak a language also called Akan.

Togo and Benin

Togo and Benin are small, hot, humid countries located on the Gulf of Guinea. Both countries are 90 percent agricultural. Almost all of the people of Togo and Benin live in villages or in the country. The crops grown there include cassava, millet, groundnuts, and palm oil. As in other countries along the Guinea Coast, coffee, cacao, and palm oil are important products. Today, Togo has large phosphate reserves. That material, used to make fertilizers, has become the nation's largest export.

The major ethnic groups in Togo are the Ewe and Kabyè. In Benin, the major groups include the Fon, the Adja, and the Fulani.

Togo was a German colony before World War I (1914-1918). After the war, Britain ruled the western half of Togo, while France ruled the eastern half. In 1957, the people of the British Togo voted to become part of Ghana. French Togo became independent in 1960.

The Drums in Ghana

The oldest and best known object in the traditions of Ghana is the drum. It is used on social, military, and political occasions for talking, dancing, and singing. Drums are carved from the trees. Most are covered with goat skin. The atumpan is a special ceremonial drum covered with elephant skin. It is large and "speaks" great distances. To be skilled with the atumpan is a great honor for a Ghanaian.

Benin was once a French **protectorate** called Dahomey. The French built a large school system but developed little of the country beyond its coast. The people of Benin rely on palm oil, peanuts, and cotton for income. At present there are not enough jobs for the people and many have left. The current name of the country comes from the Benin Kingdom that existed in West Africa during the sixteenth century.

Wildlife Preserves

Benin is also noted for its large wildlife **preserves**. The "W" National Park is a protected home for many animals native to Africa. You might see hartebeests and gazelles (two kinds of antelope), elephants, and hippopotami roaming free. The entire area of the "W" National Park covers almost three million acres of land, about half of which is located in Benin.

LESSON REVIEW

Directions: Number your paper from 1 to 5. Then answer the following questions.

1. What differences exist between developments in Ghana and the Ivory Coast since these countries gained independence?

2. How have the people of Ivory Coast attempted to improve their lives?

3. Why is the name "Ghana" important historically?

4. How have the colonial nations of Britain and France influenced the people of the Guinea Coast?

5. Why do you think the wildlife reserves are necessary in countries such as Benin?

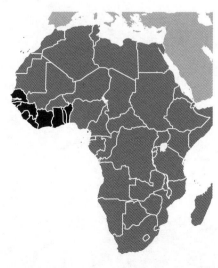

Words to Know

mahogany:
a dark tropical tree, usually yellowish to reddish brown

SPOTLIGHT STORY

Letters from Gbassie

March 15, 2000

Dear American Pen Pal,

Happy Joseph Jenkins Roberts' Birthday! That's right. In Liberia, today is a national holiday. Schools will be closed, and there will be music and dancing in the town. We are celebrating the birthday of our first African American governor, Joseph Roberts. It is much like your celebration of George Washington's birthday in the United States.

Roberts was first named Governor of Liberia 162 years ago. He took over the government from a man named Thomas Buchanan, a cousin of one of your presidents, James Buchanan. In fact, Liberia's colonial period is tied to the history of the United States. Did you know that the first colonists in Liberia were freed slaves from America? And did you know, my American friend, that our capital city, Monrovia, is named for one of your presidents, James Monroe?

Tonight Mother will cook a feast for our entire family. Our family isn't like most American families. When people in Liberia say the word *family*, they mean all of their aunts, uncles, grandparents, and cousins. More than 50 people will eat with us this evening. You should be glad that you will not be eating with us, because Liberian food is HOT—but it's actually good!

Mother will cook everything with a lot of hot peppers. Once we had a dinner guest from America. Mother made a meal of monkey meat (she sometimes uses chickens or goats), greens, and palm oil over rice. Our guest thought it looked fine—but did she ever have a surprise! I think Americans are just not used to peppers.

After supper, our whole family will go together to see our national team play a soccer game. Here in Liberia we call it football, and it is our national sport. Everyone in Liberia plays soccer!.

I will write to you again as soon as I can.

Your Liberian friend,

Gbassie

July 26, 2000

Dear American Pen Pal,

Once again I write to you on a holiday. July 26 is our Independence Day. On this date in 1847, Joseph Jenkins Roberts became the first president of the first black republic in Africa.

And on this day one year ago, my older brother John returned from "Bush School." What is Bush School, you ask? Well, Bush School is a custom of the Poro people and of the Sande people. Both are religious societies. The Poro are men, and the Sande are women. The Bush Schools teach the children the customs and traditions of the different ethnic groups.

It is very hot in Liberia. Most days I just wear a pair of shorts and maybe a T-shirt. Shoes? Sometimes. The average temperature is almost 80°F. And does it ever rain a lot. Some parts of this country get 200 inches of rain a year! With all that rain, you can imagine that there are many farmers in my country. In fact, most of the people here are farmers. They raise rice, palm trees, grapefruit, and butter pears. In your country you call butter pears "avocados."

The farmers here also export coffee, bananas, and rubber. Rubber trees look like regular trees. But when a "tapper" cuts into the tree, the sap runs out. This sap is collected and made into rubber. But the rubber isn't so important to our economy since synthetic rubber was invented.

We also have beautiful woods in Liberia. **Mahogany** and red oak grow in many of the forests. If you aren't a farmer in Liberia, you are probably a miner. There is much iron to be mined here and even some gold, diamonds, platinum, and lead.

I will write to you again soon.

Your friend,

Read the two letters from Gbassie to his pen pal. Then answer the following questions.

1. What are two holidays in Liberia?

2. Name five things that are grown in Liberia.

3. What is the name of the capital city of Liberia? Whom is it named after?

4. Describe two ways in which Liberians and Americans share a common history.

5. Tell two things about Liberia's climate.

6. Name five foods eaten in Liberia. Be sure to include a meat selection that you might find unusual.

Chapter 1 Review

The people of Coastal West Africa were the first to come in contact with the Europeans. The ten different countries of Coastal West Africa can be divided into two different regions. They are the Atlantic Coast countries and the Guinea Coast countries. All of the countries are still considered to be developing countries.

Coastal West Africa is a land of many different people. Hundreds of ethnic groups, languages, and customs exist. Yet the people of Coastal West Africa have much in common. All ten countries in this region share the same type of agriculture, history, and traditions. Cassava is grown in most of these countries, along with coffee and cacao.

Great empires like the Ghana and Ashanti have flourished. The trading of slaves was also a part of the history of West Africa. Both Siberia and Sierra Leone began as settlements for freed slaves.

These children live in Ghana, a country in Coastal West Africa.

Critical Thinking Skills

Directions: Give some thought to the questions below. Be sure to answer in complete sentences.

1. Why do you think that the official language of Guinea came to be French?

2. Why do countries like Togo and Benin rely so heavily on farming?

3. In his letters to an American pen pal, why is Gbassie so proud of Joseph Jenkins Roberts?

4. How are the farmers of Coastal West Africa different from American farmers?

For Discussion

1. If farmers from Ghana came to this country, what things would they want to take home with them?

2. Most of the countries in Coastal West Africa were once colonies of a European nation. How does this affect the way they now live?

3. Water is an especially important commodity in Africa. Think of ways in which a farmer's life is different in times of drought.

4. What popular American foods are probably not eaten in Coastal West Africa? Why not?

Write It!

Directions: Read the selection below. In a short paragraph, explain what the words of Nkrumah mean to you.

Ghana was the first colonial nation in Africa to win its independence. The area became a colony of Great Britain in 1874 and was given the name "Gold Coast." On March 6, 1957, under the leadership of Kwame Nkrumah, the Gold Coast became independent. On that day Nkrumah offered the following prophetic words:

"There is a new African in the world, ready to fight his own battles. It is the only way we can show the world we are the masters of our own destiny."

For You to Do

Directions: Make a chart of the countries of Coastal West Africa. Be sure to include population and types of government on your chart. Use colors to depict the flags of each country.

CENTRAL WEST AFRICA
CHAPTER 2

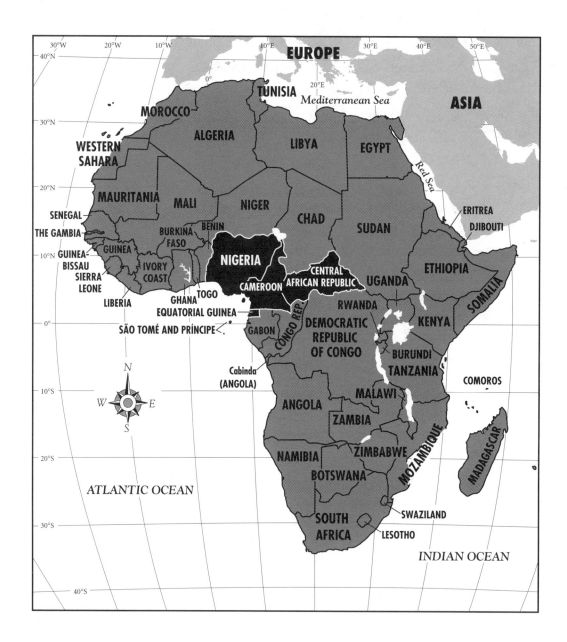

Fast Facts

- Equatorial Guinea consists of land on the mainland plus five islands.
- Cameroon has over 250 miles of coastline.
- Central African Republic has seven wildlife preserves.
- Nigeria became an independent nation in 1960.
- In Central Africa, women do the farming, and men do the hunting and fishing.

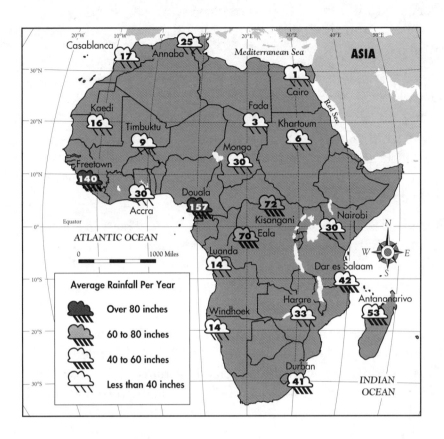

MAP SKILLS

Average Annual Rainfall in Africa

Study the map above to answer these questions.

1. What is the average amount of annual rainfall in Luanda?

2. What southern African city receives 41 inches of rainfall per year?

3. What is the average annual rainfall in Douala?

4. Which part of Africa receives the greatest amount of annual rainfall?

5. What city near the equator receives 70 inches of rain per year?

6. Which part of Africa receives the least amount of annual rainfall?

21

Words to Know

civil war:
a war between groups of people of a single area or country

delta:
the land at the mouth of a river

pollute:
to make dirty

tsetse fly:
a type of fly that carries and spreads sleeping sickness

tributary:
a branch of a river

LESSON 1: Nigeria—A Proud History

Compared with the other nations of West Africa, Nigeria is enormous. With 124 million people, it is the most populated country in all of Africa.

Nigeria extends from the wet, hot climate of the coast on the Gulf of Guinea to the dry savannas along Lake Chad. In the tropical south, palm products, cacao (seeds used to make chocolate), and rubber are grown. In the drier savannas of the north, peanuts, cotton, soybeans, and cattle are raised. However, in the central region, the **tsetse fly** and the resulting sleeping sickness prevent the development of agriculture and the raising of cattle.

Nigeria is the home of the mighty Niger River. The Niger, which has its source in the highlands of Guinea, flows for 2,600 miles. Two other major rivers are also found in Nigeria. They are the Benue, which is a **tributary**, or branch, of the Niger River, and the Komodugu-Yobe in the north.

Nigeria is one of the richest countries in Africa. Its greatest mineral resources are the large oil deposits of the Niger River **delta** region. This oil brings a new wealth to some Nigerians who work in the petroleum industry. Unfortunately, only a small portion of the people share in the wealth that oil brings. The majority of Nigerians live in villages. In fact, 50 percent of the people of Nigeria cannot read or write.

Coal deposits are also found in this delta area. Located inland are large iron ore and manganese mines. Nigeria has about half of the world's supply of columbite, a metal used in hardening steel. On the Niger River, a large hydroelectric plant has been built that will supply electric power for homes and industries.

More than two-thirds of the people are farmers. They grow yams, cassava, millet, corn, and rice as food crops. Their export crops include cacao, rubber, and palm products. Unfortunately, drought has been a serious problem for Nigeria's farmers.

For many years, Lagos was the capital city of Nigeria. However, Lagos is overcrowded, and many of its people cannot find work. Lagos is really two cities in one. The old parts of the city suffer from poor sanitary conditions and **polluted** water. The newer areas show that Lagos is a well-planned, modern city with office buildings, luxury hotels, restaurants, and universities.

The Nigerian government, aware of the problems of such an overcrowded city, changed the capital of Nigeria to a different city north and west of Lagos. Abuja is now the center of government in Nigeria.

In the north, walled cities such as Kano have been religious and trading centers for prosperous Muslim kingdoms of the past. Today, Kano is still an important cultural, religious, and trade center as well as the largest city of the north. Ibadan is another important city of southeastern Nigeria.

Nigerians Belong to Many Different Ethnic Groups

As in other African nations, Nigerians belong to many ethnic groups that have developed cultural differences. Nigerians trace their ancestry to one of more than 250 language and ethnic groups. Three major groups are the Hausa-Fulani, the Yoruba, and the Igbo.

The Yoruba of the Lagos-Ibadan region and the Igbo of the lower Niger River region of the southeast have been most influenced by the English. Many of the southern Nigerians speak English, which is the official language of the government. Most of them practice Christianity.

These schoolboys live in the village of Sokoto, Nigeria.

The Hausa-Fulani and most of the other people in the northern region are Muslims who have maintained traditional culture. In fact, about half of the people of Nigeria are Muslims. Throughout the country, however, many Nigerians combine Muslim or Christian religious practices with traditional beliefs. Their beliefs are often based on the worship of many gods and spirits. Each of the three large ethnic groups in Nigeria is distrustful of the others. Each has its own customs, religion, and language. English is the national language because it is not the language of any single group. A **civil war** broke out in 1967 when the Igbo tried to set up an independent country, Biafra. The war ended in 1970 when the Biafrans were defeated.

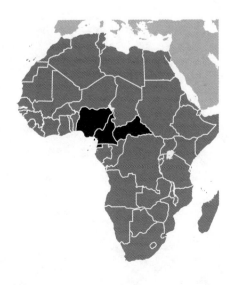

Words to Know

bronze:
a mixture of copper and another element, usually tin

terra-cotta:
a baked clay used in pottery

Culture in Nigeria

Nigeria has a proud history. Advanced cultures appeared in what is present-day Nigeria between 900 B.C. and A.D. 200. At that time, the Nok culture flourished. Working with **terra-cotta**, Nok artists sculpted nearly life-sized human figures. About A.D. 1000, the Ife made magnificent glazed pottery figures. These people also produced **bronze** portraits that rank among the world's finest sculpture. During the fourteenth century, bronze workers in Benin developed the "lost wax process" to create spectacular bronze figures and plaques. This art of early Africa has influenced many European and African artists of today.

Nok artists used terra-cotta to form human figures.

Nigerians continue to enjoy worldwide fame as skilled artists. Yoruba and Igbo artists have contributed beautiful sculpture and very high quality modern artwork to museums throughout the world.

The African "talking drum," which is found in Western Nigeria, has an hourglass shape and is covered on the top and bottom by animal skins held together with leather bands. The drummer holds the drum under his left arm and hits the top of it with a stick held in his right hand. The sounds of the drum are like the tones of speech that people use. The Igbo and the Hausa-Fulani are known for their music, instruments, and dances.

Let's Play!

The people in Nigeria are just like anyone else in Africa and in the rest of the world—they like to have fun.

Nigerians enjoy many sports, both as spectators and participants. Wrestling, soccer, polo, football (American-style), cricket, and swimming are all very popular.

Nigerians also have a love for the movies. Because most Nigerians speak English, most movies are in that language. Nigerians know all about Bill Cosby, Batman, and Freddie Kreuger. In addition to the movies, live theater and art exhibits are well attended in Nigeria. Don't forget television. Several stations currently broadcast in Nigeria.

LESSON REVIEW

Directions: Number your paper from 1 to 5. Write the correct word or words from the chapter to match each definition.

1. A branch of a major river
2. A metal used to make steel harder
3. An industry built near water to supply electric power
4. A serious problem for Nigeria's farmers
5. A method of creating bronze figures

Words to Know

ebony:
a very hard black wood

LESSON 2: Cameroon—Lowlands, Marshes, and Mountains

Cameroon is a triangle-shaped country that is located near the bend in West Africa. It has approximately 250 miles of coastline on the Gulf of Guinea. Cameroon's capital city is Yaounde. It has two official languages—English and French.

Many different types of land are located in Cameroon. You can find tropical lowlands, wooded marshes, forested mountain ranges, and grasslands. A large number of rain forests also exist in Cameroon. These tropical forests are very humid (hot and wet). They are also very dense. Within the forests, you will find plants and vines growing very close to each other. The rain forests are so dense that light can barely pass through them, and they are dark most of the time. In these vast forests grow magnificent hardwood trees like mahogany and **ebony**. Many different types of beautiful flowers also grow in Cameroon.

Wildlife Is Plentiful

This country also supports many different types of wildlife. Although hunters have made their numbers smaller, a wide variety of African animals call Cameroon their home. Some animals living in this country are rhinoceroses, monkeys of all kinds, large pythons, elephants, flying mice, and even lions. There are also crocodiles, gorillas, cheetahs, leopards, giraffes, hippopotami, buffaloes, and antelopes. Many of these animals now live on protected wildlife preserves. Cameroon has six of these preserves.

Ethnic Groups of Cameroon

Today, almost 16 million people live in Cameroon. The largest ethnic group is the Cameroon Highlanders. Other groups who live in Cameroon include the Bantu, Kirdi, and Fulani.

One group of people who are smaller than average also live in Cameroon. They are commonly known as pygmies, even though the term is incorrect. Several groups of these unique people share similar physical characteristics. The three largest groups are the Mbuti, the Akkas, and the Batwas. These people live in the forest and are primarily hunters.

Most people in this area make their living as farmers. Cameroon exports coffee, cacao, bananas, wood, cotton, tea, and rubber. Other crops include cassava, corn, rice, and sweet potatoes. Cattle are raised in the highland regions away from the coast.

Industries include bauxite, iron ore, and food processing as well as light manufacturing, lumbering, and production of crude oil.

Further development of commercial farming and mineral resources promises continued economic growth for Cameroon.

LESSON REVIEW

Directions: Number your paper from 1 to 5. Write True or False for each statement.

1. Some of Cameroon's coastline borders the Atlantic Ocean.

2. Two valuable hardwoods found in the forests of Cameroon are mahogany and ebony.

3. The official language of Cameroon is Portuguese.

4. Coffee and cacao are two important export products for Cameroon.

5. Many wild animals of Cameroon are protected on preserves.

LESSON 3: The Central African Republic and Equatorial Guinea

The Central African Republic is a poor country, even less developed than many of its neighbors. Its people suffer from many problems. Many of the citizens of the Central African Republic do not live to be 50 years old. One cause of disease and death is an insect. The tsetse fly spreads sleeping sickness, a disease that takes the lives of many of the people in this area.

Much of the Central African Republic is inhabited by wildlife. Seven wildlife preserves are in this country. The land supports great herds of antelopes, buffaloes, lions, rhinoceroses, gorillas, and elephants. Perhaps the largest remaining elephant herds in the world today can be found in the Central African Republic.

Ethnic Groups of the Central African Republic

People in the Central African Republic belong to many different ethnic groups. Among them are the Banda, the Baya, the Ubangi, the Sara, and the Mandjia. The Ubangi live along the Ubangi River, which is a chief waterway in the Central African Republic.

About 80 ethnic and language groups—most of them Bantu-speaking— make up the population of the Central African Republic. About one-fourth of the people are Roman Catholic, one-fourth are Protestant, and one-tenth are Muslim. The rest of the people practice their own traditional African religions.

Art and Literature in the Central African Republic

Many Central African artists work in watercolors and in oils. In the large villages and cities of this country, it is customary to see many paintings and murals done by local artists. These works of art can usually be seen in restaurants, bars, and other gathering places.

Jerome Ramedane is the most famous artist from this region. Ramedane's murals and canvasses often show African animal life, daily village life, and hunting parties.

Literature in Central Africa is starting to become more popular. Collectors are beginning to gather and record the region's traditional oral legends and folk tales. Pierre Makombo Bambote is the best known writer in the Central African Republic. His work is a source of great pride to the people of his country.

Many Natural Resources

The Central African Republic is trying to build up its economy. It has many natural resources, including diamonds, that have become major nonfarming industries. The country also supplies most of its own food.

Crops include cassava, potatoes, rice, sorghum, peanuts, and bananas—all of which are traded at local markets. Cotton, coffee, and sesame are cash-export crops. In addition, diamonds and timber are important export products.

Almost all of the farming in this country is done by women. The men do the hunting and fishing. In Central Africa, it is not considered honorable for a grown man to work in the fields.

Diamond mining has become a major nonfarming industry.

Akwadu (Banana-Coconut Bake)

Akwadu is a typical West African dessert. Its basic ingredients, bananas and coconuts, are both grown in the area. Just as baseball is "as American as apple pie," soccer is "as African as akwadu."

5 medium bananas

1 tablespoon butter

1/3 cup orange juice

1 tablespoon lemon juice

3 tablespoons packed brown sugar

2/3 cup shredded coconut

Cut bananas crosswise into halves; cut each piece in half. Arrange bananas in an ungreased 9-inch pie pan. Dot with butter. Drizzle with orange and lemon juice. Sprinkle with brown sugar and coconut. Heat oven to 375° and bake 8 to 10 minutes or until coconut is golden brown.

Words to Know

shaman:
a person believed to have close contact with the spirit world; medicine man

taboo:
forbidden by custom or by tradition

Equatorial Guinea

Equatorial Guinea is a very small country whose population is around a half million. Most of the people of Equatorial Guinea belong to an ethnic group known as the Bioko.

Most of the land in Equatorial Guinea contains dense rain forests. The hardwood grown there is a major product that is exported to other countries. Along the shoreline lies flat land where the people of Equatorial Guinea grow cacao, coffee, and bananas. These products are also exported.

Equatorial Guinea promotes African culture through lectures and exhibits. In the city of Bata is a museum of art that has the works of Guinea's internationally known sculptor, Leandro Mbomio.

LESSON REVIEW

Directions: Number your paper from 1 to 5. Use information from the text to help you complete the following sentences.

1. The _____ is an insect which spreads African sleeping sickness.

2. The important ____ River flows through the Central African Republic.

3. ____ may be the home of the largest herd of elephants in the world today.

4. Jerome Ramedane is a famous _____ from the Central African Republic.

5. A museum of art located in _____ displays some of the works of sculptor Leandro Mbomio.

Spotlight Story

Religion in Africa

Although many Africans are Muslims or Christians, most people still follow traditional religions. Most traditional religions profess a belief in one supreme god. However, this god in most cases can be reached only through ancestors or spirits. Many Africans believe that everything has a spirit—the trees in the forest, stones, animals, and rivers. These powerful spirits can influence people's lives. If a spirit is angry, it can take revenge.

Therefore, if a person moves a stone, he or she must be careful to do something to keep the spirit of the stone from becoming angry. Such beliefs are known as animism.

The people believe that spirits and ancestors can influence their lives. These spirits serve as the go-betweens among group members and the supreme god. The group usually makes special offerings or sacrifices to the spirit to keep its favor. There are also **taboos**. Spirits might differ in name or importance from group to group or village to village, but they are thought to be all-powerful throughout most of sub-Sahara Africa.

Magic is the idea that supernatural forces can be used by human beings. This belief is held throughout Africa. The force of magic can be used for good or evil. In Africa, most magic is used with good intent to protect persons against illness and misfortune. It promises success in farming, fishing, hunting, or even love. One important function of magic is to give people extra confidence in difficult situations.

An individual who can control this magic is of great importance and holds much power within the group. Someone who has displeased a spirit must go to a **shaman**, who is able to overpower negative or harmful forces. Traditional African belief sees a close connection between the spirit world and diseases. The shaman bridges that connection. He renames the spirit, and the person is well again. The shaman's cures, predictions, and advice are protective devices.

Traditional ethnic religions are giving way to Christianity and Islam. However, probably not more than 40 percent of sub-Saharan Africans regard themselves as either Christians or Muslims. Some converts to these religions also cling in private to traditional beliefs. Many Africans see no conflict in holding their new beliefs and their traditional beliefs at the same time.

SPOTLIGHT REVIEW

Answer the following questions.

1. What is animism?
2. What is a taboo?
3. Describe two ways in which magic is used with good intent.
4. Who is a shaman? How does the shaman help the people?
5. What is happening to traditional ethnic beliefs in Africa today? Explain your answer.

Words to Know

safari:
an expedition, usually for hunting or photographing wildlife

Chapter 2 Review

Central West Africa includes one of the largest (Nigeria) and one of the smallest (Equatorial Guinea) countries in all of Africa. Nigeria has more people than any other country in Africa. More than two-thirds of the people are farmers. The major ethnic groups are the Hausa-Fulani, the Yoruba, and the Igbo.

Cameroon is home to many kinds of wildlife. It has dense tropical forests with beautiful flowers and hardwood trees. The largest ethnic group is the Cameroon Highlanders. The Central African Republic is a very poor country. There are about 80 ethnic groups in this country. Equatorial Guinea is one of the smallest countries in Africa.

Thousands of animals roam Central West Africa.

Critical Thinking Skills

Directions: Give some thought to the questions below. Be sure to answer in complete sentences.

1. Explain why the culture of groups such as the Mbuti have remained unchanged for hundreds of years.

2. Why do you think so many animals live in the grasslands of Central West Africa?

3. Why do you think so many of the people in this area live along the banks of the Ubangi River?

4. Why are the numbers of so many wild animals getting smaller and smaller?

For Discussion

1. How do the people near the coastline live differently from those who live inland?

2. What are some of the reasons that many things grow so large and so fast in the rain forests?

3. List at least three reasons why people tend to live near a source of water.

4. In what ways is Nigeria different from its neighboring countries?

Write It!

Directions: Many Westerners take photo **safaris** to this part of the world to "shoot" the animals. Describe the animals, plants, and other natural features that a photographer might look for on the grasslands of Cameroon.

For You to Do

Directions: Go to the library to find books of recipes. Use the table of contents and the index to find traditional African recipes like akwadu. Copy these recipes. Then, tell which ingredients are easy to get and which are difficult to find in America.

Perhaps someone at home can help you prepare a recipe in traditional African style.

EQUATORIAL WEST AFRICA

CHAPTER 3

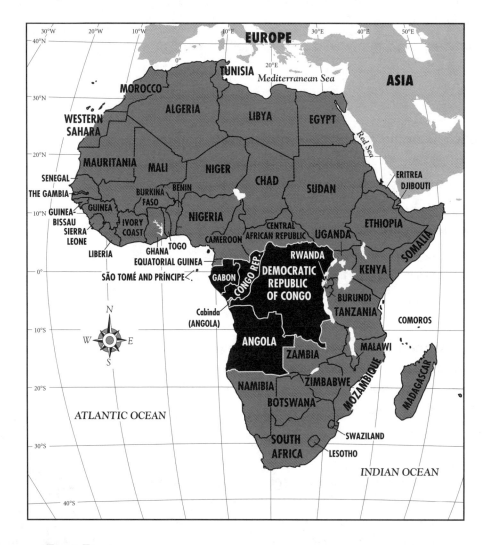

Fast Facts

• Equatorial West Africa is very rich in natural resources.

• The Congo River is the fifth longest river in the world.

• Rainfall in Gabon may reach 100 inches in a nine-month period.

• The islands of São Tomé and Príncipe are really large volcanoes rising out of the sea.

• Margherita Peak in Democratic Republic of the Congo towers 16,762 feet high.

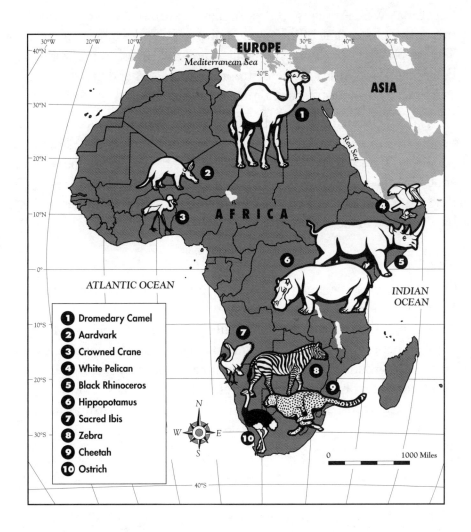

MAP SKILLS

Wildlife in Africa

Study the map above to answer these questions.

1. In what part of Africa would you find the dromedary camel?

2. In what part of Africa does the rhinoceros live?

3. What animals live in the area of South Africa?

4. Name three types of birds shown to be living in Africa.

EQUATORIAL WEST AFRICA – CHAPTER 3

Words to Know

adobe:
a building material made of sun-dried and sun-baked earth mixed with straw

dominate:
to control by strength or power

inhospitable:
not friendly or receptive; providing no shelter

silt:
dirt or sediment that is washed into and carried by rivers

uranium:
a radioactive element

LESSON 1: Land of Many Contrasts

Equatorial West Africa is an area of many contrasts. The countries in this area include some of the smallest and some of the largest in Africa. The people, too, are among the smallest and the largest in the world. In Equatorial West Africa are dense tropical rain forests and breathtaking coastlines. The countries are a mixture of poverty and wealth.

Only a few cities can be found in Equatorial Africa. Most of the people live in small villages scattered about the countryside. The people in these villages are usually farmers. The houses are made from **adobe** bricks or dried mud and sticks. Many have thatched roofs—that is, roofs made of dried bundles of grass. Wealthier families might have a house made with a tin roof.

Gabon

Gabon is a coastal country that lies almost directly on the equator. Between June and September, it rarely rains in this country. However, during the other nine months, rainfall may reach 100 inches. Much of Gabon contains thick tropical rain forests with little light; thick vines limit ground travel. As **inhospitable** as this may seem, these rain forests are a haven to many species of wild animals. Gorillas, monkeys, leopards, and tropical birds of all kinds live within the rain forests of Gabon.

The rain forests also play a major part in the economy of the area. Rich hardwoods are harvested from the rain forests. These beautiful hardwoods, such as ebony and mahogany, are the chief exports of this relatively rich nation. Other exports include cacao and coffee beans.

Additionally, the Gabonese export valuable iron, **uranium**, oil, gold, and manganese. As a result, this nation has a trade surplus. The country has been able to use the money to improve education and health care. The government of Gabon has developed a railway and roads leading to the mines and farms in the interior.

Gabon's capital city is Libreville. Approximately 350,000 people live there. Although this is a small city by American standards, it is not considered a small city by African standards. Many of the people of Gabon live in cities. This kind of population distribution is unusual for a country in Africa.

The Volcanic Islands of São Tomé and Príncipe

São Tomé and Príncipe are two small islands just off the coast of Gabon. Both are volcanic islands. They are actually large volcanoes rising out of the sea. They are about 90 miles apart. The capital city of this unique two-island nation is the city of São Tomé.

The temperature of the two islands ranges from 66°F to 77°F. This range of temperatures is perfect for growing coconuts and coffee. São Tomé and Príncipe grow a lot of cacao. Palm oil and bananas are exported to other countries.

The islands were first inhabited by the Portuguese in the fifteenth century. For many years, the islands were stopping-off points for the shipment of slaves to Western countries.

Republic of the Congo and the Congo River

Republic of the Congo is **dominated** by the Congo River. Much of the transportation, energy, and economy of this area depend on this river.

The Congo River is the largest river in Africa. However, it is not the longest river. The longest river in Africa is the Nile River. More water flows through the Congo than through the Nile. In all the world, only the Amazon River in South America carries more water. The waters of the Congo River are a rusty color. This coloring is caused by the tremendous amounts of **silt** carried by its waters.

The capital city of Republic of the Congo is Brazzaville. French was adopted as the official language in order not to favor one people's speech. However, most of the Congolese speak a Bantu language. Among these languages are Swahili, Lingala, and Mono Kutuba.

The ethnic groups of Republic of the Congo are almost all of Bantu origin. They include the Kongo, the Sangha, and the Teke. Hutus live in the rain forests of Republic of the Congo.

Republic of the Congo is a hot, humid place. Being so near the equator means that the year-round temperature is near 90°F. The tropical rain forests are rich. They are home to many types of monkeys, cobras, and pythons. Also found in the rain forests are unusual plants and valuable trees. The Congolese harvest and export oak, cedar, mahogany, and walnut trees.

Away from the rain forests, the land becomes a thick, grassy plain. This type of land, known as savanna, is home to lions, elephants, buffaloes, leopards, giraffes, and zebras.

Words to Know

sisal:
a strong white fiber used for making rope or twine

About half of the people in Republic of the Congo make their living as farmers. They raise corn, rice, and cassava. Larger farms grow and export coffee, sugarcane, and lumber.

People in Republic of the Congo mine copper, gold, and silver that are exported to other countries. The country also has oil, natural gas, and diamond deposits. Projects supported by foreign aid have built hydroelectric stations and textile mills. A shipyard in the port city of Pointe-Noire has also been built.

LESSON REVIEW

Directions: Number your paper from 1 to 5. Then answer the following questions.

1. What materials are used to build houses in Equatorial West Africa? Why are houses made with these materials?

2. What are some natural resources found in Gabon?

3. About how many years ago did the Portuguese first inhabit the islands of Príncipe and São Tomé?

4. Why is the Republic of the Congo region so hot and humid?

5. Why do you think most of the large cities of Republic of the Congo and Gabon are located either on the coast or along a river?

LESSON 2: Angola—An Uneasy Nation

Angola is one of the largest countries in Africa. However, it has one of the smallest populations, with about 11 million people living in Angola today. Many reasons contribute to this small population. For instance, in colonial times, millions of Africans were captured and sent to be traded as slaves. More recently, warfare among various political parties has kept the population of Angola small.

Of the 11 million people who live in Angola, most live on farms or in the country. Farmers produce bananas, coffee, cassava, sugarcane, and **sisal**. Sisal is used to make rope.

Angola has many natural resources. A large oil field is near Cabinda in the northwestern part of the nation. Angola also mines and exports diamonds, iron, petroleum, and gold.

Angola is a land of many rivers. Some of the rivers flow north to the Congo River, and some flow west to the Atlantic Ocean. Two of the larger rivers in Angola are the Cuazana and Cunene Rivers.

Angola Was Once the Jewel of Colonial Portugal

Hundreds of years ago, Europeans made their first contacts with people from Africa. At first, the Europeans came across the Mediterranean Sea and into Egypt.

These visitors traveled as far as the Sahara and could go no farther.

About 550 years ago, the Spanish and the Portuguese began to explore the west coast of Africa. There they discovered many riches. They found fruits, nuts, palm oil, ivory, spices, and gold. They also found a source of slave labor to send to the new world.

The Portuguese were particularly drawn to the area of what is now called Angola. They fought for centuries to make it a Portuguese colony (which it became in 1901). However, this domination of the people of western Africa did not last for long. The Angolans fought fiercely for their independence, and Angola became an independent nation in 1975.

Ethnic Differences and Civil War

Many different African ethnic groups make their homes in Angola. Unfortunately, relations among the larger groups have not always been good. Even today, in time of peace, Angolans struggle to live as one nation.

The major ethnic groups in Angola today are the Ovimbundu, the Kimbundu, and the Bakongo. Most of the members of the groups speak the Bantu language. However, Portuguese is the official language of Angola. It is spoken mainly by the remaining whites whose ancestors lived in Angola when it was a Portuguese colony.

Civil war in Angola was based on political influences and ethnic differences. In the northern part of the country, people are closely related to groups in neighboring Republic of the Congo. In the southern part of the country, people identify with groups in Namibia. The government, in the capital city of Luanda, must work hard to keep all of the people content.

After many years of war, Angolans have again begun the business of building a strong and prosperous country. Since the end of the last war, poverty levels have dropped, and Angola has made economic progress. However, troubles remain among the different ethnic groups, and people in Angola still live under a cloud of unrest.

LESSON REVIEW

Directions: Number your paper from 1 to 5. Then use the text to help you complete the following sentences.

1. Angola was at one time a colony of _____.

2. A plant product used to produce rope is _____.

3. Two important African rivers located in Angola are the _____ and _____.

4. Most of the people of Angola speak _____.

5. A war between groups of people within a single country is called a _____.

LESSON 3: Democratic Republic of the Congo— Rich in Resources

Democratic Republic of the Congo, which used to be called Zaire, is located directly on the equator. The ethnic groups of this country are almost all of Bantu origin. Although the official language is French, most people speak one of four regional languages. The nation is sometimes called Congo-Kinshasa.

This land is dependent on its largest river, the Congo River. The capital city, Kinshasa, is found along the banks of this river. The river provides transportation, energy, and water for crops.

This nation is actually made up of three different regions: the rain forest, the savannas, and the mountains.

Rain Forests

About a third of the nation is a tropical rain forest. It is much like the other rain forests that you have read about: thick, dark, and humid. Because this country is so close to the equator, its rain forest is particularly hot. The average daytime temperature in this region is 90°F.

The rain forest supports a wide variety of plant life. Beautiful hardwood trees grow there, as do palm trees and rubber trees.

Many different types of wild animals also live in the forests. Pythons, chimpanzees, and crocodiles all live within the forest.

The Savannas and Highlands

Democratic Republic of the Congo is a place of vast savannas. These wide grassy lands are dotted with small groves of trees. The grasslands make a perfect home for many of the animals you might expect to see in Africa. Herds of antelopes, zebras, buffaloes, giraffes, rhinoceroses, hippopotami, and lions live in this area.

Large areas have been set aside by the government to protect these wild animals. Hunters and a growing population are both threats to the wildlife of the area. Still, huge numbers of animals are found away from the places where people live.

The country has a mountainous highland, where summits rise over 16,000 feet. Near the eastern border is Margherita Peak. It is 16,762 feet high.

Words to Know

cobalt:
a hard, metallic element used in making alloys

Crops and Natural Resources

Democratic Republic of the Congo is rich in natural resources and has the largest hardwood reserves in Africa. Much of the land is unused. This nation also has the ability and the resources to supply electrical power for the entire country, as well as for many of its neighbors.

Most of its economic development has been focused on the mining industry. In fact, mining has become the most important economic activity. This country is one of the world's largest producers of copper. Huge, open pit copper mines can be found in the southeastern regions. Deposits of **cobalt**, gold, and tin are also found nearby. Even oil has been found off the Atlantic coast.

The nation needs money from outside sources to develop its economy. Consequently, much of the focus is on producing crops that can be exported. One exported product is palm oil, which is used as an ingredient in soap. Exported food crops include coffee and sugar.

Education Is a Priority

The goal of the country is to provide all of its citizens with a basic education. About 60 percent of the children attend a primary school. Students not only learn to read, but they also study up-to-date science and technology. Providing an education for its people is challenging for the government. There is a shortage of secondary schools, especially in the rural areas. Youths are moving to the cities in hopes of getting a good education.

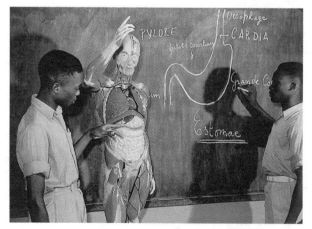

These students in Democratic Republic of the Congo are studying to be medical assistants.

Art and Music

People from all over the world are familiar with the statues, ivory carvings, masks, and jewelry of Democratic Republic of the Congo. In fact, art from all parts of the country can be found in many major museums in the world. As an individual goal, the country has made an attempt to collect and keep the art of its various groups.

Music also plays an important role in life. The people sing songs in several languages, including French and the African languages of Kongo and Luba. The most widely used language is Lingala, which is not associated with any ethnic group. Lingala used to be the official language of the army, but now it is associated only with music.

Most songs are about the daily aspects of life: love, death, lack of money, as well as world problems. One famous musician in the country is a man named Tabu Ley. He and his band, African International, have performed in the United States, Japan, and Europe.

Recent History of Democratic Republic of the Congo

Democratic Republic of the Congo was at one time called the Belgian Congo. In June of 1960, it became independent. The idea of a united country was not widely supported. The people often thought first of their own ethnic group, their own traditional culture, and the welfare of their own area. After independence, political parties battled to control the government. A civil war broke out. After several changes of government, the commander of the army, a man named Mobutu Sese Seko, took total control. Mobutu ruled the country almost until his death in 1997. Since then, the country has been very unsettled politically.

Words to Know

dowry:
money or property given by a man to or for his bride; in some cultures, it is the money or goods that a woman brings to her husband in marriage

Despite the vast base of natural resources, the government of Democratic Republic of the Congo has not been able to meet all the needs and desires of its people. As a result, the country must import consumer goods, mining and transportation equipment, and fuels. To pay for these items, the country depends on foreign loans and aid.

LESSON REVIEW

Directions: Number your paper from 1 to 5. Write True or False for each statement.

1. The Congo River plays an important role in the life of the people of the Democratic Republic of the Congo.

2. Democratic Republic of the Congo was once called the Portuguese Congo.

3. Areas located near the equator support little or no plant life.

4. Democratic Republic of the Congo has a rich tradition of art and music.

5. Democratic Republic of the Congo was peaceful after gaining its independence.

Spotlight Story

Family Life in Equatorial West Africa

Some African families include uncles, aunts, grandparents, and cousins. Some families even include more than one wife.

According to tradition, many girls in Africa are brought up differently from girls in America. African girls are brought up to be very dedicated to their husbands. They are also taught to have the highest respect for their fathers and uncles. Later, they are trained to treat all men with great respect. Until recently, girls rarely went to school. Some Africans reasoned that girls were destined to work in the fields, serve their husbands, raise a family, and run a household. Today, however, many African girls learn to read and write.

Many girls from this region marry when they are twelve years old, and most marry before they are fifteen. Sixteen-year-old girls who are still unmarried are called "old maids." It is traditional for a bride's family to receive a **dowry** when she marries. Often a young girl marries a man who already has a wife. This practice of a man having more than one wife is common in Africa.

Boys are raised differently in this part of the world too. Great importance is placed upon the traditions of the ethnic group. Boys are taught to hunt, trap, fish, and farm. They learn how to make weapons and tools, skin an animal, and find water. Storytelling is also the job of the males in African society. When they are teenagers, African boys undergo a "coming of age" ceremony. The boys are taken from their village and taught in a very intense manner about the customs and traditions of their tribe. At the end of the ceremony, each boy is considered to be a man.

SPOTLIGHT REVIEW

Answer the following questions.

1. List four traditional duties that boys are expected to fulfill in Equatorial West Africa.

2. How are the lives of young girls in Equatorial West Africa different from the lives of girls in your school?

3. How might you compare the lives of boys in Equatorial West Africa to the lives of boys in the United States?

4. Which relatives are often considered part of the African family?

5. Until recently, why were African girls usually not educated in schools?

Chapter 3 Review

Equatorial West Africa is a land of different types of people. It is a land of hot, humid rain forests and pleasant, moderately warm mountainous regions. This area is also home to many different kinds of animals.

Life is hard for the people of Equatorial West Africa. Little rainfall in some regions, bitter feuds among ethnic groups in others, and poor soil in still other areas make life difficult.

The ethnic groups of Equatorial West Africa are ancient. Their way of life has changed little in the past centuries. Farming, housing, and customs of traditional groups and families have remained unchanged, even as the industrial world has become more important.

There are few cities in Equatorial West Africa, except for Gabon. There, many people live in cities. Two small islands off the coast of Gabon, São Tomé and Príncipe, are actually large volcanoes rising out of the sea. Angola, one of the largest countries in Africa, has one of the smallest populations.

These children live in Equatorial West Africa.

Critical Thinking Skills

Directions: Give some thought to the questions below. Be sure to answer in complete sentences.

1. Why do the houses in this region so often have thatched roofs?
2. Explain why small farms grow food products, while the larger farms in the region grow rubber trees or coffee.
3. To what types of markets might the people of this region export beautiful hardwoods such as mahogany, ebony, and cedar?
4. What events explain why Angola has a small population?
5. Explain the problems that have faced the nations of this area in their search for independence.

For Discussion

1. Many of the people of Gabon live in the cities. Why is this situation unusual?
2. What are some of the things that copper is used for?
3. How are the rain forests near the Congo River different from the forests in the United States?
4. What problems might be caused in Equatorial West Africa if a dam were to be built along the Congo River?
5. How has past colonial experience affected the culture of Equatorial West Africa?

Write It!

Directions: Explain to a person in Rwanda what houses are like in the United States.

For You to Do

Directions: Make a collage of the products of Equatorial West Africa. Cut out pictures from magazines that show the products or the ways in which the products are used. To get started, try getting pictures of copper pipes, pennies, or other copper products.

SOUTH SAHARA AFRICA
CHAPTER 4

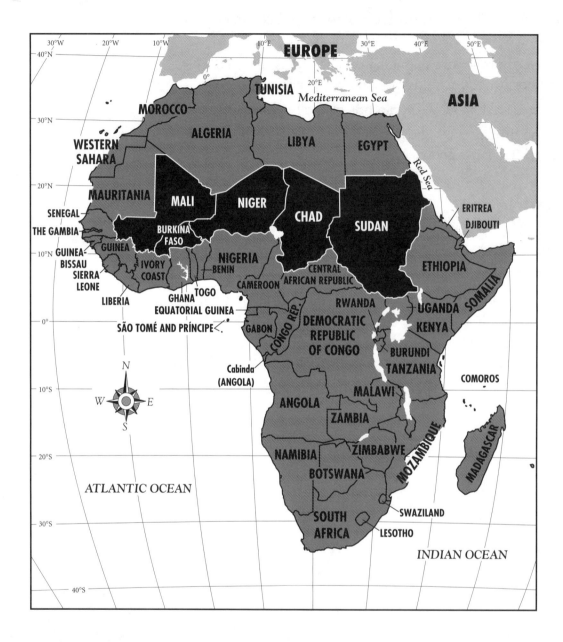

Fast Facts
- The Sahara is the largest desert in the world.
- Only three percent of the land in Niger is used to grow crops.
- Lack of rainfall has created conditions of great hardship and famine.
- The region has an important history as a route for trade.
- Temperatures in Chad and Niger often reach as high as 120°F.

MAP SKILLS

Longitude and Latitude in South Sahara Africa

Study the map above to answer these questions.

1. On what degree of longitude will you find the city of Oum Hadjer in Chad?

2. Near what degree of latitude will you find the city of Douala in Sudan?

3. What city in Niger lies at approximately 15° north latitude and 5° east longitude?

4. Through which two South Sahara countries does the Prime Meridian (0° longitude) pass?

5. Which South Sahara country has a southern border that extends to within five degrees north of the equator?

6. Which Sudanese city lies at approximately 30° east longitude?

Words to Know

gum arabic:
gum from acacia trees, used to make candy and medicine

LESSON 1: Sudan—The Nile and the Desert

Sudan is the largest country in the continent of Africa. Many different geographical features are found in this area. Much of Sudan lies on a high plateau. The country includes deserts in the north, plains spotted with grassy wetlands, and low grass savannas on the central plateau. In the wetter south are the tall grass and tree savannas.

The Nile River is the key to Sudan's economy. The great river winds through this area from south to north. Several waterfalls interrupt the smooth flow of the river. Most of Sudan's 34 million people live in the Nile Valley, a vital area that contains almost all of the country's fertile land.

Southern Sudan receives a great deal of rainfall every year. The countryside is dense with vegetation. Wildlife roam freely through the savannas. Many wild animals—including gazelles (a kind of antelope), giraffes, elephants, leopards, and lions—live in the south. The Nile is well known for its population of crocodiles and hippopotami.

Life in Sudan

About 70 percent of the Sudanese people are engaged in agricultural activities. The country's chief crop is cotton. Sudanese cotton is famous the world over for its soft quality. Other products raised in this area are peanuts, sorghum, millet, and sugarcane. Sudanese farmers account for the production of much of the world's **gum arabic**. Gum arabic comes from the acacia tree. The gum is used in candies and medicine.

About 70 percent of the people of Sudan have jobs in agriculture.

Greetings from Sudan

Hospitality is a Sudanese custom. The northern Sudanese are a formal and traditional people. However, they are very friendly in the way that they greet friends as well as strangers.

When you meet someone from Sudan, a firm but gentle handshake is usually correct. Friends often embrace. In public, men do not shake hands with, or otherwise touch, women unless the woman extends her hand first.

In northern Sudan, Arabic is widely spoken. You can expect to be greeted with *Salaam Alaykum*, meaning "peace be upon you" or *Ahlan Wa-sahlan*, meaning "welcome." You might also hear *Kayf Haalak?*, "how are you?"

Sudan's modern irrigation projects use water from the Nile River. They use the water to cultivate land and increase farm production. Using up-to-date technology has allowed the people of the Sudan to develop small deposits of oil, iron ore, gold, copper, and silver.

The political, economic, and social center of the Sudan is Khartoum. This city is located at the junction of the Blue Nile and White Nile. Khartoum is a city of modern architecture and dress, contrasting with local traditional architecture and customs. Sudan's other important cities include Omdurman, across the Nile from Khartoum, and Port Sudan on the Red Sea.

Like other countries along the southern edge of the Sahara, Sudan has been influenced by both Arab and African cultures. The Nubian people and the Arabs of the north are Islamic. They have a long history of contact with Egypt and the Middle East. The African Christians of the south have been strongly influenced by European missionaries.

After gaining independence in 1956, the government of Sudan tried to force the Islamic faith, as well as Arabic customs, on the people of the south. Since 1983, the southern region has been in rebellion against the Sudanese central government in Khartoum.

Words to Know

landlocked:
a country or place that is surrounded by land and that has no access to a sea or ocean

The Dinka of Sudan

The Dinka are a large ethnic group including about 25 major subdivisions. In all, there are about two million Dinka living across the country of Sudan. The Dinka are tall, thin people whose existence is difficult. They work hard just to survive.

Some Dinka are farmers. Usually, it is the elderly, the women, and the children who tend the farms. The more able-bodied men are herders. A man's cattle are the focus of most of his activities. Like other herders in these regions, the Dinka believe that a man's wealth is measured by how many cattle he owns.

According to Dinka traditions, cattle are more than just a symbol of wealth. They also have social and religious significance. The Dinka see a likeness in the lives of cattle and in their own lives. Cattle, to a Dinka herder, have rights of their own. They must never be killed for an unimportant reason. Thus, cattle are not killed to provide food. Sometimes cattle are sacrificed at religious ceremonies, but this act is considered an honor for the cow.

The Dinka have a keen sense of loyalty to their ethnic group. Men often take more than one wife, and some jealousy exists between wives. The wives live near each other and take turns cooking and caring for their husband.

LESSON REVIEW

Directions: Number your paper from 1 to 5. Write the reasons for the following statements.

1. Farms in the Sudan are located near the Nile River.

2. Southern Sudan has rich vegetation.

3. Khartoum is the most important city in Sudan.

4. Modern technology is important to the economic growth of Sudan.

5. The Dinka do not eat beef.

LESSON 2: Chad—A Landlocked Nation

Chad is another large country in South Sahara Africa. However, Chad is an underdeveloped, poor country because it lacks natural resources. Also, it has no access to the sea, so it's **landlocked**. Fewer than eight million people live in the entire country. The capital city of Chad is N'Djamena. The official languages of Chad are French and Arabic. However, most of the people speak Arabic in the north and a Bantu language in the south.

The northern part of Chad lies in the Sahara and is very dry. The few people who live here are Arabs or Toubou. The Toubou are an African ethnic group. The Toubou and the Arabs make their living as herders of camels, goats, cattle, and sheep.

In the south of Chad, a large number of different African ethnic groups can be found. Many of the groups are Bantu. The largest group, called the Sara, are farmers. They raise crops like millet, rice, or cassava. Larger farms in southern Chad grow cotton.

Slowly, as the desert gives way, the land becomes rich with vegetation. In the far southern part of Chad, tropical forests can be found. Wild animals—including lions, elephants, giraffes, and antelope—can be seen near the forests. A large part of Chad is a wildlife preserve. This vast area is called the Zakouma National Park.

This fishing boat, in Chad, is made from stems of the papyrus plant.

Words to Know

dictator:
a ruler who uses absolute authority or power that must be obeyed

Chad suffered through a severe drought during the 1980s. Lake Chad, once a huge lake in the middle of the country, was reduced to about one-tenth of its original size. Large areas of once-fertile land are dry and useless. Water and feed for livestock are extremely difficult to find. Many Chadians left the country in search of a better life, while others have died of malnutrition and starvation.

LESSON REVIEW

Directions: Number your paper from 1 to 5. Then use information from the text ot complete the following senteces.

1. A large part of North Chad lies in the _____.

2. An important product of farms in South Chad is _____.

3. A long period of little or no rain is called a _____.

4. One important reason why Chad is an underdeveloped country is _____.

5. The Toubou people and the Arabs make a living by _____.

LESSON 3: Burkina Faso (Upper Volta)

Burkina Faso lies between Mali and Niger to the north and the Ivory Coast to the south. Cattle raising is the traditional occupation. However, drought has reduced the number of cattle by almost 90 percent. Sleeping sickness (which is spread by the tsetse fly), famine, and other diseases have left one-third of the country without people.

Burkina Faso was once called Upper Volta by the French. The word *burkina* means "land of honest men." *Faso* means "democratic and republican." Nevertheless, the country is run by a military **dictatorship**.

Most of the 11 million people of Burkina Faso live in the few healthy and fertile areas of the south. These people earn a living as subsistence farmers. The main food crops include corn, rice, and sorghum. In addition, the country exports small amounts of peanuts and sesame seeds. Small manufacturing plants process farm products and building materials.

These herders, with their camels, stop at a watering hole.

LESSON REVIEW

Directions: Number your paper from 1 to 4. Then write the word that is described in each of the following definitions.

1. The insect that causes sleeping sickness
2. Lack of food in an area causing many people to die
3. Land that has rich soil and is capable of growing crops
4. Farmers who live and work at a level of basic existence

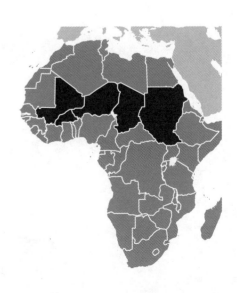

Words to Know

dialect:
a particular form of a language

goldsmith:
a person who crafts gold

nomad:
a person whose home moves from one place to another

LESSON 4: Niger—Nomads, Farmers, and Craftspeople

Niger is another large country jutting into the middle of Africa. Its northern areas are in the Sahara and support little, if any, life. Daytime temperatures in this region reach over 120°F in the spring. There is very little rainfall.

In the far southwest of this country is the Niger River. It is from this river that the country takes its name. The Niger River travels through this area for about 350 miles. Most Nigerians live along the river banks. These people depend on fishing to stay alive.

The Hausa in Niger

The capital city, Niamey, is located on the Niger River in the southwest. It is a large city of more than 600,000 people. The official language of Niger is French. However, Bantu **dialects** are spoken throughout the country.

The people of Niger belong to many different ethnic groups. The largest of these groups is the Hausa. The Hausa are mostly farmers. They raise grains such as rice, millet, and sorghum.

Other groups include the Djerma and the Tuareg. These people live in Niger only a few months of the year. During the dry season, these **nomads** go south across the border into Nigeria.

As in other parts of Africa, the people of this area are noted for their art. Nigerians are famed **goldsmiths**. They also work with leather and wood.

The people of Niger are particularly proud of their culture, which blends African ethnic tradition with Islam.

LESSON REVIEW

Directions: Number your paper from 1 to 5. Of the four terms listed, one does not belong. Can you spot the one term that does not belong? Write it on your paper.

1. Rice, millet, corn, sorghum
2. Hausa, Dinka, Djerma, Tuareg
3. Goldsmiths, fishers, farmers, dentists
4. Sahara, Nile River, Niger River, Niamey
5. Niger, Chad, Sudan, Angola

LESSON 5: Mali—Desert and Savanna

Mali sometimes seems to be two countries. The northern two-thirds lies in the Sahara and northern Sahel. The people of this region are nomads who herd cattle, sheep, goats, camels, and horses. Droughts have claimed more and more forests, causing an increased demand for firewood.

Mali has lost forests to droughts, causing a shortage of trees for firewood.

Most of the people of Mali live in the southern region, which is made up of grass savanna plains. Farmers in the south raise peanuts and sorghum for food. Cotton is raised for export. Increasing irrigation from the Niger River is Mali's hope for the future. It allows for production of rice. Numerous foreign aid projects are building dams and irrigation channels.

In Mali, the family is very important. As in most of Africa, the family is made up of all the descendants of a common ancestor. This means that uncles, aunts, grandparents, and cousins are all considered part of the family. The oldest male member of the family serves as the head of that group.

The family also consists of the spirits of all of the deceased members of that family. These spirits, it is believed, guide the living in every act of their lives.

At one time, Malian society included nobles, servants, and slaves. Today, all citizens are considered free and equal. The only distinction between people is in the type of work that they do.

Farmers are considered to be the noblest of all people, because farming implies a type of partnership with nature. People who fish, hunt, and raise cattle are considered slightly less important than farmers.

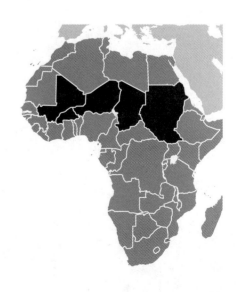

Words to Know

caste:
class or group of people

illiterate:
having little or no
education; unable to read
or write

Further down the ladder of importance are the people who work as priests or traders. Though religious leaders are respected in Mali, their lives are considered less important than those who make their living by farming or fishing.

The lowest level among groups of people include artists and craft workers. Into this **caste** fall people such as singers, musicians, historians, and storytellers or griots.

Although farmers are considered the noblest of people, they do not own land. In fact, in Mali a person does not own land in the same way that land is owned in the United States. A family may own only those things produced on the land. For example, farmers may own the corn they grow, but not the land on which it grew. No human produced the soil; therefore, no human can own it.

The actual owner of any piece of land can only use that property for producing crops or goods for the people of their village. Everyone in the village must benefit from the land. The owner is forbidden by law to destroy or sell even the smallest part of it.

LESSON REVIEW

Directions: Number your paper from 1 to 5. Then answer the following questions.

1. Why could Mali be considered two countries?

2. Why are farmers considered important in the Malian society?

3. Why does no one own land in Mali?

4. How is the family organized in Malian society?

5. Why is a belief in spirits important to the Malian people?

Spotlight Story

Education in South Sahara Africa

Many hundreds of years ago, education in South Sahara Africa meant teaching boys and girls only what they needed to know to be members of the community. Boys learned hunting, farming, and cattle herding. Girls were taught to cook, make medicines, and raise children.

As the Arabs came from the north, they tried to convert the natives to become Muslims. They brought teachers, called marabouts, to the area. These marabouts were responsible for educating the Africans about Islam.

In the twentieth century, Western churches sent missionaries to South Sahara Africa. The Protestants and the Catholics attempted to convert the Africans to their religions. These missionaries taught the people how to read and write.

Today, about one-fourth of the citizens are able to read and write. There are many reasons for this. One reason is that many of the children of Sudan, Chad, Mali, and other countries are nomads. The government has not yet found a way to set up schools for these wanderers. Another reason is expense. Education costs a lot of money. These countries are very poor— among the poorest in the world.

A third reason is that the children are needed at home. Their parents do not allow them to attend school. Boys are needed to tend the fields or to help with the herds. Girls are needed to help with household chores and with younger children.

A fourth reason is that religious and traditional beliefs teach that girls should not be educated. Many Africans believe that girls should stay at home and prepare to become wives and mothers.

Education in this part of the world is of great importance. For many reasons, however, the children of the countries of South Sahara Africa are among the most **illiterate** people in the world.

SPOTLIGHT REVIEW

Answer the following questions.

1. Before the Arabs came to this area, what things did the natives teach their children?

2. What things did the Arab teachers consider important for the Africans to learn?

3. What were the Arab teachers called?

4. What two Western groups sent missionaries to this area?

5. List four reasons why education is so difficult in this part of the world.

Chapter 4 Review

South Sahara Africa is dominated by the Sahara. Making a living and raising a family in this part of the world are never easy. Still, many people make South Sahara Africa their home. They fish, farm, and herd cattle.

Sudan is the largest country in the continent of Africa. The Nile River is the key to Sudan's economy, and most of the people live in the Nile Valley. Sudan has been influenced by both Arab and African cultures. Many different ethnic groups live in the country. One large ethnic group living in Sudan is the Dinka. Chad has few natural resources, and no access to the sea. There is a large wildlife preserve in Chad.

Most Nigerians live along the banks of the Niger River. The largest ethnic group in Nigeria is the Hausa. The Nigerians are famous for their work with gold. The people who live in the northern two-thirds of Mali are nomads. The people in the southern region of Mali are farmers.

South Sahara Africa is dominated by the Sahara.

Critical Thinking Skills

Directions: Give some thought to the questions below. Be sure to answer in complete sentences.

1. Why do you think Khartoum, the capital city of Sudan, is located at the meeting point of two rivers?

2. How do you think the farmers in this region survive in years of drought?

3. What would you do if you lived in Burkina Faso and were unable to feed your family?

4. Why do you think the government of Chad provides a national park to protect wildlife?

For Discussion

1. If rainfall is so scarce in South Sahara Africa, why don't the people move elsewhere?

2. What part of a nomad's life seems to be desirable? What part seems to be undesirable?

3. What are some reasons that people in this area are not able to read and write?

Write It!

Imagine that you are a farmer in northern Mali. For the past 15 years, the drought has persisted and the land has become drier and drier. How would you describe your situation to an American farmer in Iowa?

For You to Do

Directions: Research Native Americans. They were often nomads, just as some groups in South Sahara Africa are nomads. However, various groups traveled from place to place for different reasons. Find out why many groups of Native Americans were nomads.

SOUTHERN AFRICA
CHAPTER 5

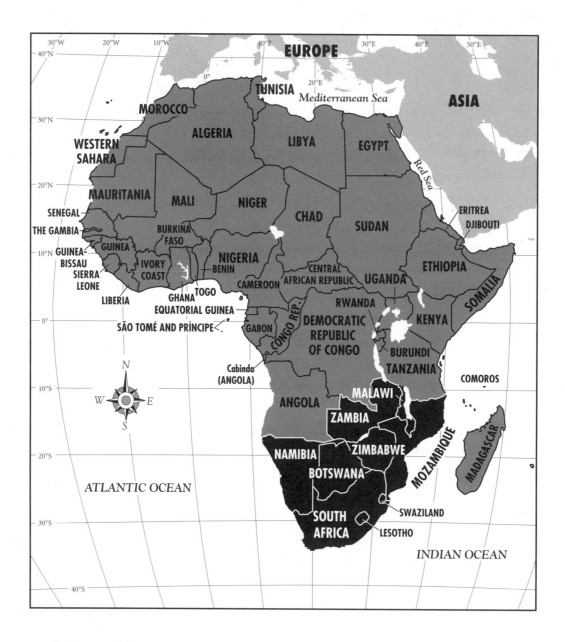

Fast Facts

• During the rainy season, more than one million gallons of water per second drop over Victoria Falls.

• The vast Okavango swamps in Botswana are full of amazing wildlife.

• Southern Africa is a storehouse of minerals, gold, and diamonds.

• In Swaziland, a man's wealth is measured by the number of cattle he owns.

• Zimbabwe contains ruins of an ancient city built over 1,000 years ago.

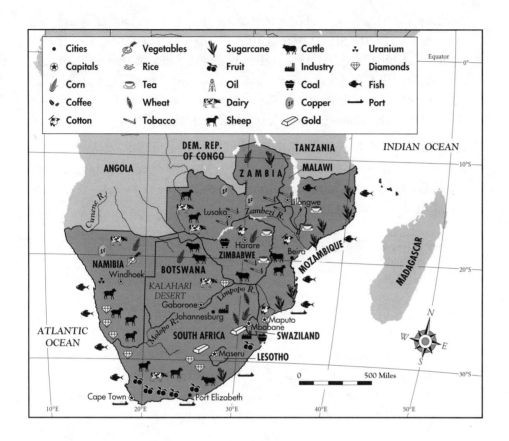

MAP SKILLS

Product Map of Southern Africa

Study the map above to answer these questions.

1. What two products can be found in Botswana near the Kalahari Desert?

2. Near what port city in South Africa might you find a lot of fruit?

3. Name four products found in Namibia.

4. In which country can you expect to find gold mines?

5. What cash crop is grown near the Zambesi River in Zambia?

LESSON 1: The Republic of South Africa

Southern Africa is a land dominated by the country called South Africa. South Africa is different from many of the countries in this book. The biggest difference is that it was the last of the African nations to allow blacks to participate in government. Though almost 90 percent of South Africans are non-white, people of European descent ran the country until just a few years ago.

Another way that South Africa is different from other African countries is its wealth. South Africa is a great source of diamonds and gold. These exports have made South Africa one of the richest, most developed nations in the world.

South Africa: The Wealthiest Nation on the Continent

The Republic of South Africa is located on the very southern tip of Africa. It is one of the most remarkable countries in the world. Its land area covers only about 4 percent of the African continent. Only about 6 percent of the people of Africa live in the Republic of South Africa. Yet the Republic of South Africa produces 40 percent of the manufactured goods in Africa, 50 percent of its minerals, and 20 percent of all its farm products. The Republic of South Africa is by far the wealthiest nation in all of Africa. It produces the largest amount of gold and the second largest amount of diamonds of any country in the world. It is also the leading African producer of automobiles, electricity, machinery, and many other goods.

The Geography of South Africa

The Republic of South Africa lies at the southern end of the African continent. It is made up of four provinces (Cape, Natal, Transvaal, and Orange Free State). It is the only country in Africa that lies almost entirely in the region that is called the Temperate Zone (Middle Latitudes—22° south to 35° south).

Except for a narrow coastal plain, the country is mainly a great plateau. The western and northern parts of the plateau are desert. The rest is a grassy prairie land, known as a veld. The highveld is a large area of high plains and grasslands located in the east central interior. The bushveld is a savanna of short trees and bushes at lower levels. The lowveld includes a dry, tall tree savanna and the moist forest found near the coastal plain.

The Ethnic Groups of South Africa

South Africa contains an interesting mixture of people. It is a country of almost 44 million people of four different ethnic backgrounds. Less than 2 percent (6 million) of the population of South Africa is of Indian descent. Most of the Indians living in South Africa came from India to work on huge sugarcane plantations.

The largest group in South Africa is made up of 33 million blacks. Many are descendants of Bantu ethnic groups such as the Zulu or the Xhosa. Others are from the Sotho and Tswana ethnic groups.

About four million people of mixed race form a third group, called "colored," in South Africa. These people are a mix of black African, white, or Asian races.

A fourth group in South Africa is the whites. Of the five million or so white people in South Africa, most are Afrikaners. This term applies to the descendants of the Dutch, German, and French who settled in South Africa in the seventeenth and eighteenth centuries.

History of European Settlement

For about 200 years before the arrival of the Dutch in 1652, groups of Africans had been migrating into the area. These people are known as Bantu-speaking people because they spoke languages that were similar. However, their cultures and histories were very different. Non-Bantu groups, such as the Khoikhoi, or Hottentots, also lived in the area.

The Zulu were one of these Bantu groups who migrated to South Africa. By the early nineteenth century, Zulu King Shaka had built a strong military empire. He developed new methods of warfare and reorganized his army into a powerful fighting force. He successfully expanded the Zulu empire into much of modern-day South Africa.

The building of this empire resulted in many changes. The people defeated by the Zulu left their traditional home and moved north, forcing still other groups farther north.

At about the same time, fateful events were taking place to the south of the Zulu empire. In 1652, the Dutch East India Company sent colonists to the southern tip of South Africa. The colonists were to grow vegetables and raise cattle to be sold to the ships traveling between Europe and India and the East Indies. The Cape Colony, as it was called, became very successful.

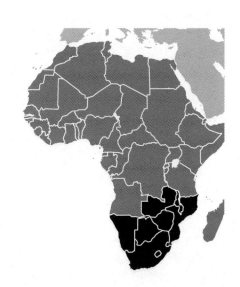

Words to Know

apartheid:
a system of race relations, officially used in South Africa 1948-94, whereby the races were separated in power and status, with whites dominating blacks

discriminate:
to treat one person or group of people better than another

guerilla:
people who attack an enemy suddenly, who are not members of a regular army

sanction:
economic measure used to force a country to change its behavior or laws

The Dutch settlers were known as Boers, which in Dutch means "farmers." They are the ancestors of about 70 percent of modern white South Africans, who are today known as Afrikaners. The Boer language is called Afrikaans, which is made up of the African, old Dutch, and Malay languages.

In the early 1800s, the British took control of the Cape Colony and its main city, Cape Town. The Boers disliked the English, and they showed their resentment by leaving. Loading all of their belongings, along with their families, into wagons, they set out for land north of the Cape. It was at this time that the European Boers came into contact with the expanding Zulu empire and the migrating Bantu-speaking people.

When the Boers began their Great Trek or migration north in 1836, they met few native Africans. This area, north of the Orange River, had recently lost a large part of its population. Wars had killed many people. Some were hiding, and still others had moved because of normal nomadic custom.

The Boers set up two independent countries—the Orange Free State and the Transvaal. At the same time (1843), the English established the colony of Natal on the coast of the Indian Ocean.

The Boers soon came into conflict with the Zulu. The two groups fought for over 40 years for control of the land. The Zulu were first victorious over the Boers but were then defeated by them.

In 1867 diamonds were found near Kimberly in the Orange Free State. Later, the world's largest gold deposits were found near Johannesburg in the Transvaal. The discovery of these gold deposits brought a large number of English settlers to the Boer Republics. In 1879, the British became involved in the Boer-Zulu wars. The Zulu defeated the British in several battles, but superior weapons and armies eventually led to the British destruction of the Zulu empire. At the same time, the British defeated the Xhosa and the Tswana, two other ethnic groups of South Africa.

The discovery of diamonds and gold brought thousands of British, while other Europeans also invaded the area. In 1899, hostile feelings between the British and the Boers broke out in the South African War, also called the Boer War. The Boers used **guerilla** warfare, and the British set up concentration camps in which many Boer civilians died. This bitter war continued for three years. Finally, in 1902, the Boers surrendered.

In 1910 the British created the Union of South Africa. A Boer leader was named manager to make sure that the white Boer minority would maintain control. During the next four decades, an unofficial policy of racial separation existed.

In the 1948 elections, the government of South Africa came under the control of the Nationalist Party. The Nationalist Party's goals were to set up, by law, the separation of the races. This goal was accomplished through a policy of **apartheid**.

The idea of apartheid was that each race was to improve its own culture and future. However, the apartheid laws were used to reinforce Boer (Afrikaner) privilege, power, and wealth.

Apartheid Grips South Africa

Apartheid once brought international attention to South Africa. Although whites never numbered more than 15 percent of the population, they controlled the government until 1994. Black South Africans, Asians, and people of mixed race were not allowed to participate in the government.

Apartheid means "separateness" in Afrikaans, one of South Africa's official languages. In reality, it meant **discrimination** against all nonwhite people. It meant that black South Africans, Asians, and people of mixed race were not allowed to live in the same areas as whites, send their children to the same schools, or even swim on the same beaches. Apartheid in South Africa was very much like the discrimination that blacks faced in the United States before the Civil Rights movement.

In 1912 four young lawyers, all black, formed the South African Native National Congress. The purpose of this political party was to unite all the blacks of South Africa in an effort to protest against apartheid. This party later became the African National Congress (ANC).

Apartheid first became the official government policy in 1948. In the 1980s, the system of apartheid—and the country of South Africa—was condemned by almost every other nation in the world. South Africa was cut off from the rest of the world by **sanctions**. Some countries refused to trade with South Africa, and some refused to recognize the government of South Africa. Such sanctions hurt the country economically. They were used against South Africa in an attempt to get the government to change its policy of apartheid.

Words to Know

homelands:
territory on which black South Africans had to live under the system of apartheid

township:
a residential area established to house black South Africans who are kept from having homes in urban areas

A Long Way to Go

But the problems in South Africa did not go away. For years, blacks, Asians, and people of mixed descent had been discriminated against. Only whites were allowed to live in the prosperous cities of South Africa. Nonwhites were often forced to live in special territories called **homelands**. The homelands were on lands that the white-run government did not want. Minerals, natural resources, and good soil for growing crops were reserved for places where white people lived.

Some nonwhites lived in **townships**. Townships were located near mines or factories so that the mine owners and factory owners could get workers. But blacks, Asians, and people of mixed descent were not allowed a share in the mines and factories.

Because of the way that the wealth of South Africa was kept among only one group of people, the other groups are still poor today. Blacks in South Africa are just now beginning to show economic improvement. The Afrikaners still control much of South Africa's wealth.

The transfer of power from white South Africans to black South Africans was remarkable. Many people believed such a change would not come peacefully, but only through a bloody revolution. The ability of Nelson Mandela to forgive and work with white people was a big factor in this peaceful change.

After this change, a national Truth and Reconciliation Commission was established. It gave people a chance to admit bad things they had done under apartheid without being punished. Archbishop Desmond Tutu was head of this commission. A black South African, he received a Nobel Peace Prize in 1984 for his work toward peaceful change in his country.

Nelson Mandela

There were also forces working within South Africa to end apartheid. Nelson Mandela, one of the leaders of the ANC, is a particularly important name in the history of South Africa. Mandela was a leader of the ANC when the movement was just beginning to gain popularity.

In 1956 Mandela was charged with high treason. In 1961 he was found not guilty of the charges. But the police still suspected him of organizing black protests against the policies of the South African government. Mandela was arrested again in August of 1962 and was imprisoned on Robben Island. The island had been used as a prison for many years. This time he was found guilty of encouraging the people to strike and of leaving the country without documents. He was sentenced to five years in prison.

Mandela was not defeated. He continued to be a leader of his people even from prison. The government of South Africa attempted to silence Mandela and in 1964 convicted him of high treason. Mandela was sentenced to life in prison.

Mandela's story did not end in 1964. In 1990, at the age of 71, he was released from prison by F. W. de Klerk, the president of South Africa. Sanctions imposed by most of the world had affected the government of South Africa. Upon his release, Mandela proclaimed his dedication to the struggle of the blacks of South Africa. "Our march to freedom is irreversible," he said. "We must not allow fear to stand in our way."

Nelson Mandela

By 1994, the pressures on South Africa both from within and from abroad were great. Apartheid was abolished in 1994. A free election was held and blacks, Asians, and people of mixed descent were allowed to vote for the very first time in South African history. The ANC won nearly two of every three seats in the National Assembly. The Assembly voted Nelson Mandela the first black president of South Africa. He served until the election of 1999, when he retired.

Words to Know

urban:
relating to a city

Ways of Life

When we look at the way in which South Africans live, we need to look at each group separately. The whites of South Africa are chiefly an **urban** group. Their homes, dress, and foods are much like what you would expect to see in any American city. One difference is that many whites in this country employ black South Africans as servants. Such help exists because so much cheap labor is available.

Most Asians and people of mixed race live in the cities of South Africa. The majority of these people work in low-paying jobs. Many are servants, factory workers, or plantation workers.

Work is scarce for many of the blacks in South Africa. Many black men are unskilled laborers and must travel to find work. Their families are rarely permitted to go with them.

LESSON REVIEW

Directions: Number your paper from 1 to 5. Choose from the list of words to complete the sentences. Write the complete sentence on your paper.

apartheid	Zulu	Boers
townships	Xhosa	homelands

1. Dutch settlers were known as _____, which means "farmers."

2. Sections for black workers connected to white cities were called _____.

3. Special territories with poor land created for blacks to live in were called _____.

4. Two large ethnic groups who lived in South Africa were the _____ and the _____.

5. The system of separate race relations in South Africa was called _____.

LESSON 2: Namibia—The Road to Independence

Namibia is located along the Atlantic coast to the west and north of South Africa. Before 1919 Namibia was a German colony, German Southwest Africa. During World War I (1914-18), soldiers from the Union of South Africa drove out the Germans. After that, South Africa ruled the area.

Namibia is a very dry country. Along the coast is the Namib Desert. The name *Namibia* means "land of the Namib." Farther east and inland is the Kalahari Desert. Most of the people live in northern Namibia, where the climate is cooler and not as dry.

The people of Namibia—both black and white—earn their living through ranching. They also raise cattle and sheep on the savanna and in the highlands. Fishing along the Atlantic Coast is also an important source of income. However, Namibia's mineral resources provide the greatest sources of jobs. Along the coast in the south are large diamond deposits. In the savanna and uplands, large deposits of uranium, copper, lead, and zinc are mined.

Apartheid was introduced into Namibia at the same time that it was introduced into South Africa. As a result, even though 90 percent of the population was black, the government and wealth were controlled by Afrikaners and other whites from South Africa. The legislature was controlled by whites.

Beginning in the late 1970s, Namibian black rebel groups began fighting for the independence of the area. The rebels attacked South African troops from bases in Angola. South African troops, in turn, attacked rebel bases that were inside South Angola. Discussions between the rebels and representatives of South Africa took place throughout the 1980s. In 1988 an agreement was reached in regard to independence for Namibia. In November of 1989, an assembly was elected to write a constitution for the new country. Finally, in March 1990, a final agreement was signed at the United Nations, granting Namibia its independence.

LESSON REVIEW

Directions: Number your paper from 1 to 5. Write the word *true* if the statement is true. Write the word *false* if the statement is false.

1. Few, if any, mineral resources exist in Namibia.

2. The Namib and Kalahari deserts are important parts of Namibia.

3. Apartheid was never introduced into Namibia.

4. Namibia was once ruled by Germany.

5. The Namibians have been unsuccessful in their struggle for independence.

Words to Know

asbestos:
mineral that does not burn or conduct heat

eucalyptus:
an evergreen tree with useful wood, gums, resins, and oils

LESSON 3: Swaziland, Botswana, Lesotho

Swaziland is a beautiful country surrounded on three sides by South Africa. Its neighbor to the northeast is Mozambique. It is a land of rich, fertile soil and has many natural resources and minerals. Large forests dot the countryside, and beautiful mountains accent the land.

Despite all of its riches, the people of Swaziland are mostly peasant farmers. This situation exists because almost half of the land in Swaziland is owned by outsiders, mainly South Africans and white Europeans.

The Swazi of Swaziland

Almost all (90 percent) of the people of Swaziland are black. Of these people, 95 percent are from an ethnic group called the Swazi—a people of Bantu origin. The Swazi are noted for their highly developed warrior system. They were once regarded as fierce enemies by others in the region. This has made Swaziland a united country. The Swazis have a common language and traditions. The rules of law and government are based on Swazi traditional customs.

The Swazi regard cattle as valuable property. In fact, when a Swazi man marries, he must pay his bride's family in cattle. A man's wealth in Swaziland is often measured by how many cattle he owns. A farmer with a large herd is respected by other men, yet cattle are rarely slaughtered and used for food. Instead, they are traded or sold for cash. The Swazi also use cattle for religious ceremonies.

In Swaziland, a man's wealth is often measured by how may cattle he owns.

In addition to raising cattle, Swazi farmers grow a number of crops. A Swazi farm might include fields of cassava, rice, or corn. Larger farms are usually owned by South Africans. These plantations grow crops to export. These crops include pineapples, sugarcane, and tobacco. An unusual crop in Swaziland is the **eucalyptus** tree. Plantation owners have planted eucalyptus forests in the mountainous areas of Swaziland. These wooded areas are among the largest forests that people have planted in Africa.

Farms, mines, and businesses in South Africa employ about one-third of Swaziland's workers. Most workers spend at least six months a year working in South Africa. The rest of the labor force works in small, local mining and lumbering operations. Swaziland is fortunate in having mineral resources: coal, **asbestos**, iron, and lumber.

About half of Swaziland's trade is with South Africa. It also has access to the sea through part of Maputo in neighboring Mozambique.

Mbabane: Capital of Swaziland

The capital city of Swaziland is Mbabane. In Swazi towns and cities, most of the people live in houses much like you would see in an American city. In the countryside, the people usually live in huts arranged in homesteads. A homestead is a group of huts in which a single extended family might live. Since a Swazi man may have more than one wife, the homesteads are sometimes quite large.

Botswana

Botswana was the former British territory of Bechuanaland. Botswana lies north of South Africa, between Namibia and Zimbabwe. It is an arid, landlocked country about the size of the state of Texas. Much of the country lies on a high plateau in the Kalahari Desert.

The British took control of Botswana in 1866 to connect the Cape with Rhodesia (Zimbabwe and Zambia) and to avoid the Boers in the Transvaal. The British invested little in the area. At the time of independence in 1966, there were no paved roads or electricity and only one important factory, a meat-canning plant.

Today, about 75 percent of Botswana's workers farm or raise cattle. The main food products include corn, sorghum, millet, black-eyed peas, and cattle. Mineral deposits of diamonds, copper, nickel, and coal provide jobs and income. Most exports and imports must come through South Africa.

About 1.5 million people live in Botswana. The major ethnic group is the Tswana (almost 95 percent of the people). English is the official language, but only one-fourth of the people speak it. Most people also speak Tswana.

Most of Botswana's people live along the wetter eastern area. Within the Kalahari live the San and the Khoikhoi, who are nomadic hunters and gatherers.

Education in Lesotho

The school systems in Lesotho are very much like the school systems in Europe. In fact, Lesotho's schools are patterned after those in Great Britain.

All children may attend an elementary school for seven years. Each year is called a "standard."

After completing seven standards, the children of Lesotho take an examination. If the student passes the examination and the parents can afford tuition, secondary education can begin. After another three years and another exam, a Junior Certificate is given.

Lesotho

Lesotho is completely surrounded by the Republic of South Africa. Very little land is suitable for farming. However, its rugged land has protected them from attack. A tradition of independence prevented the kingdom from being included in South Africa.

Most of Lesotho's 2.2 million people live in small villages. More than 95 percent are members of the Sotho, a Bantu group. Traditionally, the Sotho live in communities arranged around a kraal, where cattle are kept. The English word *corral* comes from the Sesotho "kraal."

Lesotho has few natural resources and almost no level land. That's why many people leave Lesotho to work in the mines of South Africa. All imported and exported products such as diamonds, wool, and food must be sent through South Africa. These factors make it very difficult for this small nation to become truly independent.

LESSON REVIEW

Directions: Number your paper from 1 to 5. Write *Lesotho*, *Botswana*, *Swaziland*, or *All* for each statement to identify the country to which it refers.

1. It is completely surrounded by the Republic of South Africa.

2. It was once a colony of Great Britain.

3. Cattle raising is an important source of food and income.

4. An important uniting factor is that it's one very large ethnic group.

5. Mining provides products for export and jobs.

When this picture was taken in Johannesburg, South Africa, the people still lived under apartheid.

Words to Know

dynasty:
a group or family that rules from one generation to the next

LESSON 4: Zimbabwe, Zambia, Malawi

Zimbabwe is a country that takes its name from ancient inhabitants. More than five hundred years ago, a great and powerful people, the Karanga, lived in this area. Karanga **dynasties** ruled much of the land in what is now Zimbabwe, Mozambique, and Zambia. The Karanga word for capital city or enclosure was "Zimbabwe." Their largest city, the Great Zimbabwe, was located in what is now the southern part of this country. The ancient ruins are still there, a marvel and a mystery to all who visit. These ruins are a symbol of the achievements of African cultures before the arrival of the Europeans.

Over a hundred years ago, Zimbabwe was called Matabeleland. That's because it was inhabited by a Bantu ethnic group called the Matabele. In the 1880s, a man named Cecil Rhodes forced the Matabele to surrender ownership of their land to the British.

Matabeleland, along with what is now called Zambia, became a country called Rhodesia. Then, at the end of the century, Rhodesia became two countries: Southern Rhodesia and Northern Rhodesia. After the Africans won a struggle with white supremacy rule similar to South Africa's in April of 1980, Southern Rhodesia became the independent country of Zimbabwe. Northern Rhodesia became the independent country of Zambia.

The Geography of Zimbabwe

Zimbabwe is a breathtakingly beautiful country, shaped like a bowl turned upside down. The middle part of the country is a high plateau. The edges of Zimbabwe are lower lands. The country is landlocked with Mozambique to its east, Botswana to its west, Zambia to its north, and the Republic of South Africa to its south.

Zimbabwe extends from the dry savanna along the Limpopo River in the south to the tree savannas along the Zambesi River in the north. Most of this area is a highland plateau of rolling plains and hills. The climates are mild, and the soils are rich.

About 80 percent of the people farm. They raise tobacco, tea, sugarcane, cotton, and corn. Zimbabwe is free of the tsetse fly, so herders raise cattle and sheep for meat. The country also has large deposits of copper, gold, asbestos, and coal.

The capital of Zimbabwe is Harare. The official language in Zimbabwe is English, but most people speak one of the Bantu languages. Large numbers of the Matabele still live in Zimbabwe. Sometimes the Matabele are called the Ndebele. The largest ethnic group in the country is Mashona.

Zambia: Copper Is King

Zambia, formerly Northern Rhodesia, is located north of Zimbabwe. It has a similar history. It became an independent country in 1964, 16 years before Zimbabwe.

Zambia takes its name from the great Zambesi River. The magnificent, world-famous Victoria Falls is located on this river. It is one of the most spectacular sights in the world.

The capital city is Lusaka. Once again, as in Zimbabwe, the official language is English. However, almost all Zambians are of Bantu origin and speak one of the ethnic dialects. The largest ethnic groups in Zambia are the Tonga, the Barotse, the Ila, and the Bemba.

Though located near the equator, Zambia has a mild climate. That is because Zambia is mostly in an area of high altitude. Being up in the mountains also allows Zambians to grow many different kinds of crops.

The chief industry in Zambia involves copper. Copper mines have attracted many workers who, until recently, have been farmers. Growth in mining has caused the cities of Zambia to grow very quickly.

Victoria Falls

In the native language, Victoria Falls is called Mosi-oa-tunya. That name means "the smoke that thunders." During the rainy season, which lasts from March to May, over one million gallons of water drop over the falls per second! The splashing water sends a smoke-like spray hundreds of feet into the air. The deafening roar of the water sounds just like thunder!

Victoria Falls is almost one mile wide and 350 feet high. That's over twice the height and twice the width of Niagara Falls. Victoria Falls is fed by the Zambesi River system. It is one of the largest tourist attractions in the area. At the bottom of the falls, tourist boats must share the waters with crocodiles and hippopotami.

As the people leave the farms, they move toward the cities near the copper mining areas. Zambia also exports cobalt, lead, emeralds, and uranium. The mining industry provides not only jobs for Zambians but also much of the government's income.

Farming in Zambia

Farmers in Zambia live much the same as farmers in the neighboring countries. Farmers work small plots of land that are right next to their houses. Their houses are usually simple, circular in design, and made from mud. The roofs are made of dried grass bundled together.

Zambian farmers grow corn, sorghum, cassava, and peanuts. Farmers with access to the roads and railroads grow peanuts, cotton, tobacco, and corn for export. The Zambian government is trying to improve agriculture in the rural areas, away from the roads and railroads, by developing cooperative farms.

Religion in Malawi

About three-quarters of the people are Christian. But many Malawians also follow traditional African religious beliefs. These beliefs revolve around the idea that all things—whether they be alive or dead, human or animal—are part of a vital life force. Relatives and rulers who have died are thought to watch over family and village affairs. These beliefs are sometimes called animism. About 15 percent of the people in Malawi are Muslims, followers of the Islamic religion.

Malawi

Malawi was once known as Nyasaland. Malawi is landlocked between Zambia to the west and Mozambique to the east. Lake Nyasa fills much of the valley and forms most of Malawi's eastern border. Its climate is moderate, even though it is near the equator. That's because of the high altitude of Malawi. This moderate climate and plentiful rainfall make conditions in Malawi ideal for farming.

Bantu people make up 95 percent of Malawi's population. The chief ethnic groups include the Chewa, Nyanja, and the Ngoni. Malawi became independent from Great Britain in 1964. English and Chichewa, a traditional Bantu language, are the official languages of the country.

Malawi has about ten million people. Most of them are farmers. Export crops include coffee, tobacco, tea, sugarcane, peanuts, and cotton. Crops raised for food on a local basis are corn, cassava, and potatoes, along with other grains. Malawi lacks mineral resources, and even today manufacturing remains very limited.

Malawi's main problem is its location. Like all landlocked countries, Malawi depends on its neighbors for the safe passage of its imports and exports.

Malawi's major resources are its wildlife, its agriculture, Lake Malawi, and its beautiful, forested highlands and mountains. Large game preserves have been created in many parts of the country. With new roads and hotels, Malawi could profit greatly from tourism.

LESSON REVIEW

Directions: Number your paper from 1 to 5. Then answer the following questions.

1. Why are the ruins of the Great Zimbabwe important to history?

2. Why have the people of Zimbabwe been able to raise cattle and sheep?

3. Why do the people of Zambia build their huts of mud and dry grass?

4. Why is copper "king" in Zambia?

5. Why is Malawi's location a problem?

Words to Know

copra:
the dried meat of coconuts; coconut oil comes from copra

LESSON 5: Mozambique

Mozambique has many harbors located on the southeast coast of Africa. It is a tropical country with a typical warm climate. Very little information is available on Mozambique until about the fifteenth century. At that time, the Karanga, under the leadership of Mwene Mutapa, ruled all of the area.

It is known that Arabs had been sailing to Mozambique for many years. The Karanga and the Arabs had developed a strong trade relationship with the area. The Arabs brought woven cloth, glass, tools, and beads to trade. In return, they received ivory, gold, rhinoceros horns, and slaves. The trade between the Karanga and Arabs was very successful. By the 1400s great markets existed solely for the purpose of trading with Arab sea captains.

Then, in the second half of the fifteenth century, Vasco da Gama set sail from Portugal and landed in Mozambique. Da Gama reported back to the Portuguese that there was great wealth to be had in Mozambique. By 1629, the area of what is now Mozambique became a Portuguese colony.

The people of Mozambique are almost all black Africans of Banti origin. Two of the largest ethnic groups in Mozambique are the Makua and the Chokwe.

Most of the people in Mozambique earn a living as farmers. The land is good for growing because the area is near the ocean and receives plenty of rainfall. The main obstacle to farming is the dense tropical forest that takes up much of the usable land.

Farmland in this area is cleared by the "slash and burn" farming method. This method of cutting down trees and burning the remaining brush has been used for centuries. However, the method robs the soil of its nutrients and its ability to keep water. Slash and burn farming quickly tires out the soil so more and more land is needed to farm.

Mozambique's Natural Resouces

Mozambique has abundant natural resources for development. Good farmland covers about one-third of the land area, and water resources are plentiful. The farmers produce tea, sugarcane, rice, cotton, cashew nuts, sisal, and **copra**. As more land is developed and newer farming methods are developed, other cash crops can be raised.

There are deposits of coal (which is rare in Africa), iron ore, bauxite, and asbestos. The export of these minerals adds strength to Mozambique's economy.

These workers are grinding rice at a farm cooperative in Mozambique.

A Luta Continua!

In Portuguese, the official language of Mozambique, the phrase *A Luta Continua* means "The struggle continues." The struggle began in 1962 when the people of Mozambique banded together to throw out their colonial rulers, the Portuguese.

Under the Portuguese, conditions were very bad for the people of Mozambique. Most people were not able to get proper health care, food, clothing, housing, or education. Civil unrest has made improvements difficult.

Mozambique has been an independent country only since 1975. Although improvement has been made, leaders of Mozambique know that more must be done for the people. *A Luta Continua!*

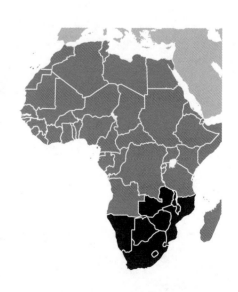

Words to Know

invincible:
incapable of being conquered

tactic:
system or planned procedure

The Economy of Mozambique

The general economy of Mozambique is not well developed. Farming is the major source of income. Industry is limited to oil refining and food processing. Some Mozambicans earn a living catching fish and shrimp from the Indian Ocean. Many men leave their homes for months at a time to find work in South Africa.

Neighboring countries such as South Africa, Zimbabwe, Swaziland, and Malawi all use Mozambique's railways and port facilities. The country receives a fee for the usage.

LESSON REVIEW

Directions: Number your paper from 1 to 5. Change one word in each sentence to make it true.

1. The people of Mozambique fish in the Pacific Ocean.

2. In 1629 Mozambique became a French colony.

3. Most of the people of Mozambique earn a living in mining.

4. The dried meat of the coconut is called sisal.

5. The major ethnic group of Mozambique is the Portuguese.

These Zulu men are wearing traditional ceremonial dress.

Spotlight Story

The Zulu

Without a doubt, the most widely known ethnic group in all of Africa is the Zulu.

The Zulu are a Bantu people. Members of this group live mainly in South Africa. About half of the Zulu in South Africa live in a township called KwaZulu-Natal. Sometimes this area is referred to as Zululand.

The Zulu people are famous for being fierce warriors. This reputation came to the Zulu under the rule of a king called Shaka. Shaka was the son of a Zulu chief. His mother took him from his village to be raised by the Mthetwa, a warlike people.

Soon, Shaka grew to be a capable warrior and leader. When Shaka's father died, Shaka returned to the Zulu and took command of them by force.

Under Shaka's rule, the Zulu nation expanded. He trained thousands of warriors and molded them into an **invincible** army. Shaka devised new battle **tactics** and invented new weapons. He proved to the Zulu warriors that the throwing spear that they used was useless. Instead, he commanded his armies to carry short spears used for stabbing.

Shaka was murdered by his own brothers in 1828. He had ruled the Zulu for twelve years. During that time, he had become a cruel and hated ruler. However, he also had become the leader of a great and powerful nation. Fifty years after Shaka's death, the Zulu were still the largest and fiercest nation of black Africans.

As the British moved into Zululand, they met with tremendous resistance. In 1879, an enormous British army was sent to capture the Zulu chief and crush his armies. Only 55 British soldiers survived. The Zulu used their stabbing spears to defeat the British army. However, in further battles, the guns and cannons of the British overpowered the spears and shields of the Zulu. The chief was captured, and the Zulu army was defeated.

The Zulu nation was confined to Zululand and governed first by the British and then by the South Africans. For many years, the Zulu ethnic group suffered under the hardships of apartheid. Still, these proud people hold on to their traditions and their customs.

SPOTLIGHT REVIEW

Answer the following questions.

1. What weapon did Shaka introduce to the Zulu warriors?
2. Where do most of the Zulu people live today?
3. What group in the history of the United States reminds you of the Zulu experience in Africa?
4. What army eventually defeated the Zulu?

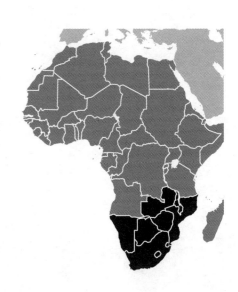

Chapter 5 Review

Southern Africa is a breathtakingly beautiful land. Its towering mountain ranges, inspirational waterways, and broad plateaus make it a marvelous spot for tourists to visit. It is also a land of great potential wealth. Vast amounts of gold, diamonds, uranium, and copper are hidden in the ground. Cattle thrive in great numbers.

Dutch settlers, known as Boers, are the ancestors of about 70 percent of modern white South Africans. South Africa was the last of the African nations to allow blacks to participate in government. Apartheid, a system where whites dominated nonwhites in South Africa, was the official government policy until 1994. Nelson Mandela was an important figure in the transfer of power from white South Africans to black South Africans and the end of apartheid.

The country of Lesotho is completely surrounded by South Africa. Swaziland is surrounded on three sides by South Africa, and on the fourth side by Mozambique. The Zulu is the best-known ethnic group in Africa.

These children, members of the Zulu tribe, live near Durban, South Africa.

Critical Thinking Skills

Directions: Give some thought to the questions below. Be sure to answer in complete sentences.

1. Why couldn't the neighbors of the Republic of South Africa refuse to import goods from South Africa?

2. In what ways was the Republic of South Africa dependent on its neighbors?

3. Why do you think cattle are so important to the men in Zimbabwe?

4. In what ways are the Zulus like the Native Americans in the United States?

For Discussion

1. Why do you think the people of Swaziland do not eat cattle?

2. What part or parts of the United States once had laws separating blacks and whites?

3. Describe some reasons that Swaziland and Namibia are dependent upon the Republic of South Africa.

4. Explain why slash and burn farming is a "short-term solution to a long-term problem."

Write It!

Directions: Imagine that you were in the Zulu army during the rule of Shaka. How would you describe your days in a letter to your best friend?

For You To Do

Directions: In Mozambique, the "slash and burn" farming method has been used for centuries. With this method, brush and grasses are burned off after the crops have been harvested. Trees are cut down. This uses up the nutrients in the soil and makes the soil less able to soak up water.

Research some different methods that farmers might use to avoid harming the soil, such as "rotating crops." Rotating crops refers to the practice of planting a different crop in a piece of land each season. Each crop takes different nutrients from the soil.

EASTERN AFRICA
CHAPTER 6

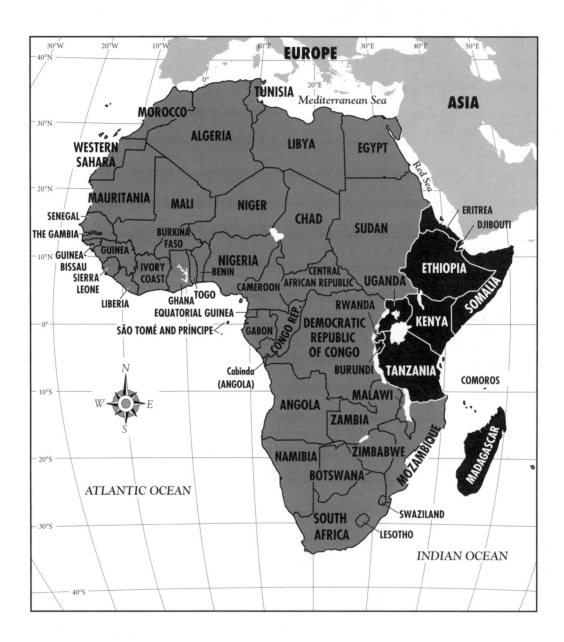

Fast Facts

- Termite mounds in Somalia can be 30 feet high.
- Mt. Kilimanjaro, at 19,340 feet, is the highest mountain in Africa.
- Somalia's official language did not have a written form until 1971.
- Uganda is famous for its large number of crocodiles.
- Most of the islands of Comoros were formed by volcanoes.

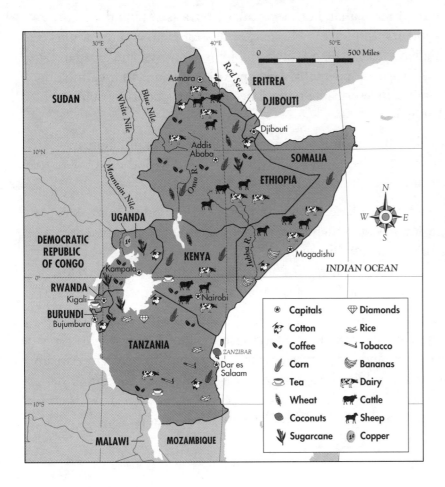

MAP SKILLS

Products of Eastern Africa

Study the map above to answer these questions.

1. What are the two main products of Somalia?

2. In which country are coconuts grown?

3. What two products are grown in Burundi?

4. Which of these is not found in Ethiopia: diamonds, cotton, coffee, or wheat?

5. What nonfood crop is grown in Tanzania near the Indian Ocean?

6. What three crops are grown along the Omo River?

EASTERN AFRICA – CHAPTER 6

Words to Know

escarpment:
sharp, steep cliffs

fossil:
traces of earlier life forms
preserved in rock

intermarriage:
marriage of persons of
different ethnic or religious
groups

landform:
a physical feature of the
earth's surface, such as
plains, plateaus, hills or
mountains

LESSON 1: Beautiful Land, Suffering People

Eastern Africa is a land of spectacular contrasts. Along the coast, **escarpments** tower above the narrow coastal plain and the waters of the Indian Ocean. Inland, highland forests, deserts, and grassland form the varied topography. Eastern Africa is a land of breathtaking mountains, indescribable natural beauties, and countless numbers of wild animals.

Tragically, the region is also one of terrible poverty and human suffering. Drought, famine, and civil war clash with the beauty of the people and the physical setting.

Narrow coast lowlands dominate Eastern Africa on the east. Most of the region lies on a high plateau that begins at the escarpment. Magnificent mountains such as Mt. Kilimanjaro (19,340 feet), Mt. Kirinyaga or Mt. Kenya (17,058 feet), and Mt. Elgon (14,178 feet) rise high above the floor of the plateau.

The Rift Valley is the most important feature of the geography. It is perhaps the most remarkable **landform** in all of Africa. The rift was formed thousands of years ago when a section of the Eastern African plateau dropped down to form a narrow valley floor. Rainwater has filled parts of the valley and created several great lakes. Lake Victoria, Lake Tanganyika, and Lake Malawi are three examples.

LESSON REVIEW

Directions: Number your paper from 1 to 5. Then answer the following questions.

1. Why can Eastern Africa be called a "land of spectacular contrasts"?
2. What makes the Rift Valley remarkable?
3. Why is there so much poverty in Eastern Africa?
4. How were Lakes Victoria, Tanganyika, and Malawi created?
5. What are the names of some mountains in this part of Africa? Which is the highest?

LESSON 2: Tanzania—Land of Contrasts

Tanzania is the largest country in Eastern Africa. It consists of two separate areas that came together in 1964—mainland Tanganyika and the island of Zanzibar, located in the Indian Ocean off the east coast of Africa.

Mainland Tanzania is a plateau country covered by tall-tree savannas. The greatest landform in Tanzania is the snowcapped Mt. Kilimanjaro, located near the border with Kenya. The mountain's southern slopes are a rich agricultural region, due to the rainfall and excellent soil.

The Rift Valley also passes through Tanzania. The famous Serengeti Plain is located here.

In addition to the geographical wonders of Tanzania, the government has set aside a huge game preserve called the Serengeti National Park. Tens of thousands of visitors come each year to see the huge herds of gazelles, elephants, buffaloes, and zebras. In 1987 an aerial photograph of Serengeti showed more than a million animals living within the park.

Near the Serengeti Plain is the famous Olduvai Gorge, where some of the oldest human **fossils** known to exist have been discovered.

Tanzania was once a British colony. Through the efforts of Julius Nyerere and other nationalists, it gained its independence from Great Britain in 1961.

Tanzania's Ethnic Groups

Over 100 ethnic groups contribute to Tanzania's cultural makeup. Bantu-speaking groups account for the majority of the country's 31 million people. The largest ethnic groups are the Sukuma, the Nyamwezi, and the Makonde.

One large nomadic group, the Masai, herds cattle, sheep, and goats along a strip of highland that extends from Kenya far into Tanzania. In this area, Masai herders burn the original vegetation in order to create open grasslands to graze their cattle.

Along the coast and on the island of Zanzibar, most of the people are of Arabic background. These traditional Islamic societies maintain a culture that is very different from that of the plateau peoples.

Intermarriage between Arabs, who came to the area as traders and merchants, and the local Bantu people occurred widely. The combining of these two groups created a culture that was a mix of African and Arab traditions. The new culture brought about a new language—Swahili. Today, Swahili is spoken by most people throughout East Africa.

Arabs and Swahili both live in Zanzibar.

Small Farms and Local Factories

Tanzania is a country of small farms. Corn, peas, beans, and wheat are the main food crops. The main cash-export crops are sisal, coffee, and cotton. Zanzibar produces nearly all of the world's cloves. Copra is also an export of Zanzibar. However, Tanzania has one very serious problem that interferes with its development. Half of the country is full of tsetse flies. Few people can live in these areas.

Tanzania has many minerals, including diamonds, gold, coal, iron ore, nickel, and natural gas. Unfortunately, these deposits are neither large nor rich.

Most of Tanzania's factories make goods for local markets. Examples include food processing, oil refining, building materials, and textiles. Dar es Salaam is Tanzania's chief manufacturing center as well as its capital and main port. *Dar es Salaam* means "haven of peace" in Arabic. However, there are plans to move the capital to Dodoma.

Tanzanians are noted for their carvings. They are most famous for their African masks used in religious ceremonies. Museums all over the world display masks carved by the Makonde of Tanzania.

The Masai of East Africa

The Masai are a people living in most parts of Eastern Africa. They are excellent cattle herders and treat their cattle with great respect.

Curiously enough, these expert cattle herders often don't have enough food. The Masai believe that a man is judged by how many cattle he owns. For this reason, Masai herders do not slaughter and eat the cattle. Instead, they raise cattle and sell off part of their herd from time to time.

The men of the Masai are also known as hunters. Warriors prove their bravery by hunting and killing a lion. They do the hunting armed with only a spear and a shield.

Masai women also are well known in Africa for their shaved heads and their iron and copper jewelry.

LESSON REVIEW

Directions: Number your paper from 1 to 5. Then answer the following questions.

1. Where does the name "Tanzania" come from?

2. Why is the Olduvai Gorge an important place?

3. What is the history of the Swahili language?

4. What kind of carvings are Tanzanians known for?

5. Why don't Masai herders kill and eat their cattle?

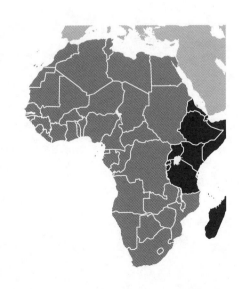

Words to Know

anthropologist:
a person who studies the science of humankind and compares human cultures

LESSON 3: Uganda—An Early Civilization

Uganda is a story of a once great country that fell into poverty. Civilization in East Africa may have begun in the country that is now called Uganda. Evidence of prehistoric tools is found in this area. Proof exists that animals were tamed and raised here before anywhere else in this part of the world.

Anthropologists and historians point to Uganda as the place where many farming methods were first used. As the years passed, the people who lived in Uganda created great kingdoms. People from many other parts of Africa came to live in Uganda.

Today, many different ethnic groups live in this country. Bantu ethnic groups live in Southern Uganda: the Buganda, the Busoga, and the Toro. Other ethnic groups include the Acholi, the Lango, and the Karamajong.

The capital city of Uganda is Kampala. The official language is English. However, most of the people speak a native language.

Most of Uganda lies on a high plateau. It is a nation of lakes, which cover nearly one-third of the country's area. Lakes Victoria, Albert, Kyoga, George, and Edward all fall partially or entirely within Uganda. The tall-tree savanna topography, good soil, and adequate rainfall make farming the main occupation. Coffee, tea, tobacco, cotton, and bananas are the leading cash crops. The main food crops are sweet potatoes, cassava, corn, and beans. Cattle are another source of food.

There are copper and tin deposits to be developed. Great dams have been built on the Nile River; they provide cheap and abundant power. With all these advantages, Uganda had great potential to develop into a world-class economy. However, in 1971 Idi Amin Dada became president of Uganda and became a powerful dictator. He ordered 40,000 to 50,000 well-educated Ugandans and Asians to leave the country.

Amin also invaded Tanzania in 1978. This act brought about a counter-invasion by the Tanzanian armies. Eventually, Amin was driven from the country. By that time, however, Uganda's economy had fallen into ruin.

Rebuilding Uganda has not been easy. Ethnic disputes between rival groups continue. However, Uganda's great agricultural potential still remains.

Uganda is a beautiful place, despite its problems. There are areas of beautiful scenery, snowcapped mountains, and thick tropical forests. The waters are famous for their many hippopotami and crocodiles. Many other kinds of wildlife also live there.

At night the river banks in this area can be dangerous. Hippopotami come on land to eat grass. During a nighttime feeding, they will usually stay close to water but may wander as far as 25 miles away. Watch out! A startled hippopotamus can run at speeds up to 25 miles per hour.

LESSON REVIEW

Directions: Number your paper from 1 to 4. Answer the following questions *True* or *False*.

1. Most of Uganda is in a river valley.

2. Idi Amin did much to improve life in Uganda.

3. Uganda can be called a "nation of lakes."

4. Uganda has great agricultural development potential.

Words to Know

exotic:
wildly different or unusual to the beholder

heritage:
traditions inherited or passed down from one generation to another

calabash:
a type of gourd

LESSON 4: Kenya—People and Animals

Kenya stretches from the Indian Ocean to the Great Rift Valley. It includes marshy coastal lowlands, a dry grassy central plain, and a western highland plateau. Kenya's people are unevenly distributed throughout the country. Because the northern part of Kenya suffers from a shortage of water, more than 80 percent of the people live in the south. Only 13 percent of the land is suitable for agriculture. In the north, Somali and Galla herders move across large areas in search of grazing lands. In the south, the Masai do the same.

Agriculture in the highlands is increasingly concentrated on small farms. The key cash crops are coffee, tea, cotton, sugarcane, and sisal. The food crops are sorghum, corn, wheat, rice, and cassava. Kenyan farmers raise enough food to feed the people of Kenya.

Unlike many African countries, Kenya does not have many mineral resources. Therefore, its industry produces textiles, paper, plastics, soap, and processed food, mainly for local use. Many factories have been built in Kenya's two major cities—the capital, Nairobi, and the main port, Mombasa. Both of these modern cities are centers of the tourist trade, which has become a major source of income for Kenya.

The plains of Kenya are densely populated by wild animal life. Much of the land in Kenya's plains has been set aside as wildlife preserves. On and off of these preserves live **exotic** African wildlife. Elephants, cheetahs, lions, rhinoceroses, hartebeests (a kind of antelope), buffaloes, giraffes, zebras, and other species share this vast land. Crocodiles, hippopotami, ostriches, storks, eagles, and other exotic birds also live in Kenya.

Many people travel to Kenya to see wild animals. Safaris hunt, track, photograph, and just watch tremendous numbers of animals that most people see only one at a time in a zoo or a circus.

History of Kenya

Kenya's first cities were founded by Arab and Portuguese traders and merchants along the coast of the Indian Ocean. The traders went inland to trade for ivory and slaves. In the sixteenth century, they gained control of the coastal cities. During the nineteenth century, the British built a railroad from Mombasa on the coast to Lake Victoria far inland. In the Kenyan highlands, the British built large, productive farms. Along with the British settlers came workers from India and Pakistan. The local Kikuyu people had little choice but to move to other areas or become farm workers.

In the years following World War II, Kenyans protested British colonial rule. There were peaceful demonstrations as well as outbreaks of violence by a group called the Mau Mau. The Mau Mau was a secret guerilla organization made up of Kikuyu people, led by Jomo Kenyatta. At the heart of this conflict were arguments about the rights to land.

Finally, in 1963, after a bloody revolt and civil war as Africans fought with Africans, Kenya became independent. Jomo Kenyatta became Kenya's first president.

Most Kenyans trace their **heritage** to one of the nearly 40 ethnic groups that live in Kenya today. The largest group, the Kikuyu, makes up 21 percent of the people.

Both Europeans and Arabs, with their different religious beliefs and languages, contribute to Kenya's cultural makeup. About two-thirds of the people are Christian, and 7 percent are Muslims. Swahili serves as the official language of Kenya, although it is not the language of any one African tribe. Swahili includes a mixture of words from Bantu languages, Arabic, Portuguese, and English.

Almost 29 million people live in Kenya today. The country is growing very fast. One reason for this growth in population is that, in Kenya, a man's success in life is measured by how many children he has. Kenyans also have large families because of necessity—it is usually farmers' sons and daughters who work the farm.

Kenyans are known the world over as loyal and honest people. When a person from Kenya promises something, it is like a sacred oath.

Calabashes and More

Kenyans are famous for their many art forms. Decorated **calabashes**, or gourds, are a product of the Kamba, a south Kenyan ethnic group. Calabashes are carved into containers, cooking pots, and musical instruments. In addition, Masai women are famous for their beautiful beadwork.

LESSON REVIEW

Directions: Of the four terms listed, one does not belong. Can you spot the one term that does not belong? Write it on your paper.

1. Geography: Lake Victoria, Indian Ocean, Mt. Kenya, Atlantic Ocean

2. People: Kikuyu, Masai, Galla, Mau Mau

3. Languages: Swahili, English, French, Arabic

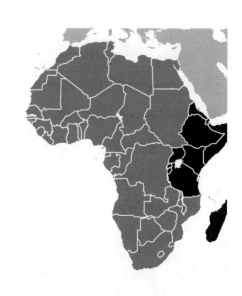

LESSON 5: Rwanda and Burundi— Mountains Near the Equator

Rwanda and Burundi are two very small nations in the middle of Africa. These two countries share a common climate, population, and history. Both Rwanda and Burundi are located very close to the equator. Still, they both have pleasant, cool climates because the countries are located in a mountainous region. The capital of Burundi is Bujumbura, and the capital city of Rwanda is Kigali.

Both countries are extremely poor. Few industries and only a small amount of natural resources exist. Transportation of goods in or out of the area is very expensive. That's because of the difficult terrain and the distance from any waterways. In both countries, most of the people make their living as farmers. Even as farmers, the people of Burundi and Rwanda have serious problems. Both of these countries are crowded. Land is scarce. What little land there is has poor soil. That's a result of the unsuitable farming techniques used and because of erosion. Crops in this area include coffee, bananas, cassava, beans, tea, and sweet potatoes.

The crops grown in Rwanda and Burundi depend on the altitude. For example, farmers raise a type of coffee called robusta on land less than 5,000 feet above sea level. Robusta is used mainly for making instant coffee. On the other hand, when the mountains rise above 5,000 feet, the coffee grown is called arabica. This arabica coffee is used for regular brewing. Both arabica and robusta coffees are grown for export.

The coffee grown high in the mountains must be sent by boat to cities in neighboring countries, like the Republic of the Congo and Tanzania. This long journey causes the prices to be very high. Coffee from this area of Africa is very expensive, and very little of the money goes to the farmer.

These workers are picking tea on a tea plantation.

LESSON REVIEW

Directions: Number your paper from 1 to 5. Write *Yes* if the statement is true about BOTH Rwanda and Burundi. Write *No* if it is not.

1. Geography influences farming.

2. Natural resources make up a large part of their exports.

3. Coffee is an important cash crop.

4. Modern, well-maintained roads make transportation simple.

5. Close to the equator, but climate is cool and pleasant.

This woman in Kigali, Rwanda, is carrying bananas on her head—and a passenger on her back.

LESSON 6: Ethiopia—A Land of Ancient People

The capital city of Ethiopia is Addis Ababa. The city includes a mix of modern architecture and mud houses. The official language of Ethiopia is Amharic.

Some of the oldest fossils of human beings were discovered in Ethiopia. Some fossils are over three million years old. Many scientists dig for fossils in this area, hoping to find clues to the beginning of humans on the earth. In 1974 Donald Johanson, an American anthropologist working in the Afar region in Ethiopia, discovered a skeleton of a pre-human female. This creature, nicknamed "Lucy," apparently walked upright on the African plains more than three million years ago.

Today, Ethiopia is made up of many different ethnic groups. Often these groups do not get along with one another. One result is a poor country where thousands of people die of starvation each year.

Poverty is widespread among all of the groups in Ethiopia. Poor farming methods, severe drought, and war between ethnic groups have made Ethiopia one of the poorest nations in the world. Also, much of the good soil they need to grow their crops gets blown away. Both humans and animals suffer.

The Ethnic Groups of Ethiopia

Ethiopia has many nomadic groups. These nomads raise cattle and depend upon rain to produce grazing lands for their herds. Many Somalis also travel through this country.

Semites are people who come from Middle Eastern or Arab countries. In Ethiopia, most of the Semites are from Arabia and speak a language called Ge'ez. Semites have been a major influence on the Ethiopian government for many years.

The Amharics have also been an important part of the government. These people are from the mountainous areas of the country.

The Galla, the Shankali, and the Falashas are other groups of considerable size in Ethiopia. Each group maintains its own heritage.

The Falashas are Jews. This group of black Hebrews claims to be descended from a lost tribe of Moses. Recently, many Falashas have left Ethiopia. They were aided by the Israeli Jews and taken to Israel.

The Land

Ethiopia lies north of Kenya. It includes very dry lowlands along its borders and a central plateau crisscrossed by mountains. When there is abundant rainfall, the fertile soil makes the plateau—home to most Ethiopians—ideal for farming. In the dry lowlands, herders and their flocks follow the rains in search of grazing lands.

Drought and famine have affected people and animals in Ethiopia.

Under the Fly in Eastern Africa

Many parts of Eastern Africa are said to be "under the fly." The fly is the tsetse fly, which causes widespread sickness and death among humans and cattle.

The tsetse fly is a medium-sized flying insect with a deep and painful bite. It carries a germ that causes sleeping sickness. The disease is fatal to humans if not treated promptly. In this part of Africa, doctors and medicine are very scarce.

Areas that are infested with tsetse flies are very dangerous. The insects swarm in clouds and can completely cover a cow or a human. Their sharp sting can even penetrate clothing.

Controlling the tsetse fly is possible. Insecticides are effective against this insect. Uganda sprayed over three million acres of land with insecticide and practically rid the country of the fly. However, spraying is very expensive. At the present time, many areas in Eastern Africa remain full of tsetse flies. Signs warn, "You Are Now Entering a Tsetse Fly Area." It is a good idea to heed the warning.

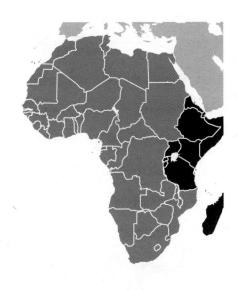

When Visiting in Ethiopia

An Ethiopian home is a very private, personal place where no one is expected to visit without an invitation. Visitors should bring a small gift when visiting for the first time.

Visitors are expected to sample some sort of food or drink. To refuse is considered to be quite rude. In Ethiopia, the host takes great pride in offering guests the best meal possible. It is customary to give a visitor more food than he or she could possibly eat.

But don't worry. It is also considered polite to leave some food on your plate. To your host, this act will mean that you have satisfied your appetite.

Farming and Industry

Geographers believe that coffee was first used as a drink in Ethiopia. Today, coffee ranks as a major export. Farmers in Ethiopia also grow many different cereal crops. However, Ethiopians cannot grow nearly enough food to feed themselves. Great amounts of foreign aid are needed every year for the people to survive. Still, thousands have died from starvation due to a severe drought and the resulting famine.

Industrial development is very limited in Ethiopia. Small factories in the capital of Addis Ababa provide goods for local markets.

A Long History of Independence

Ethiopia is one of the oldest countries in the world. At one time, the influence of Ethiopia spread all the way to India in the east and to Greece in the north. It is also one of the oldest Christian nations in the world.

Many times in the past centuries, the people of this country have been invaded by outsiders. Arabs and Europeans have tried many times to conquer the people of Ethiopia. Only once were they successful. In 1935 Italy conquered and governed Ethiopia. However, the Italians were forced out six years later.

Since the days of the powerful ancient kingdom of Aksum, Ethiopia's history has often been one of quarreling small states. A ruling class—including the royal family and the Christian (Coptic) Church—held most of the economic and political power. Most of the people were very poor. In 1974 a combination of drought, student unrest, and years of resentment led to a revolution. The Emperor Haile Selassie, who had ruled since 1917, was overthrown. A military dictatorship built on a Communist model was set up. Ethiopians rebelled against this government in the early 1990s.

Revolt in Eritrea

Some of Ethiopia's many ethnic groups have threatened to break away from the country. The people of Eritrea (a separate country that formerly was part of Ethiopia) are made up of many ethnic groups. However, they are Muslims and have little in common with the Christians.

A long struggle for independence ended when Eritrea declared itself a separate nation in 1993. Ethiopia and Eritrea have fought several brief wars since then, and the border is still in dispute.

LESSON REVIEW

Directions: Number your paper from 1 to 5. Then answer the following questions.

1. Who was "Lucy"?
2. Who are the Falashas?
3. What is the tsetse fly?
4. What is Addis Ababa?
5. What is Eritrea?

LESSON 7: Djibouti and Somalia

Djibouti is a small country located at the entrance to the Red Sea. The area has extremely high temperatures. Although it is almost too hot to be inhabited, it has a deep harbor on the Red Sea.

Fewer than 500,000 people live in all of Djibouti, most of them in the capital city. They are divided into two different ethnic groups of nomads, the Afars and the Somali. Neither of these ethnic groups lives well.

The capital city of Djibouti is also called Djibouti. It has a few bottling plants and a harbor. No other industries or manufacturing plants exist. Most of the people in the city of Djibouti are poor.

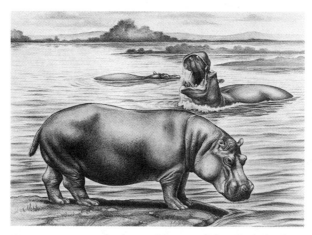

Hippopatami and other wild animals live in Somalia.

Somalia, Land of the Nomads

In Somalia, temperatures frequently rise above 100°F. It is also a dry land where very few crops can grow. Because of the conditions in Somalia, most of its people are nomads. They wander from place to place in search of grazing lands for their livestock. Livestock in Somalia almost always means cattle. However, some nomads will keep herds of goats, sheep, or camels.

The nomadic groups in Somalia are the Somali and the Bantu. Along the banks of the Jubba and the Shabeelle Rivers, they grow sugarcane, corn, and bananas. Lions, giraffes, hippopotami, and other wild animals live in Somalia. The capital of Somalia is Mogadishu.

Somalians, as a group, are highly respected as poets. Even though the Somali people have only recently adopted a written language, the children of Somalia are raised to respect the spoken word.

The Acacia Tree

A strange tree called the acacia tree grows in Somalia. Its roots grow very deep into the soil to search for water. Its leaves spread wide to provide shade in an otherwise shadeless place. Wild animals like goats or antelope try to eat the leaves of the acacia tree. To do this, they must stand on their hind legs and be careful not to chew the sharp thorns of the tree.

Other interesting trees also grow in Somalia. The baobab tree, and fragrant trees such as frankincense and myrrh, grow in this region. These fragrant trees grow in the very driest parts of the country.

The combination of very dry weather and occasional wet seasons creates a perfect condition for termites. Termite columns in Somalia are a sight to behold. Often a traveler in the middle of the desert will come upon a termite mound that is 15 feet high!

LESSON REVIEW

Directions: Number your paper from 1 to 5. Change *one* word in each sentence to make the statement true. Then write the new sentence on your paper.

1. Djibouti has an important harbor on the Black Sea.
2. The people of Djibouti belong mainly to the Afar and Issa nomadic groups.
3. The Somali and Jubba are the nomads of Somalia.
4. Asmara is the capital of Somalia.
5. There are many unusual trees in Somalia.

Words to Know

strategic:
necessary or important to
carry out a plan

LESSON 8: Indian Ocean Islands

Four island nations—Madagascar, Comoros, Seychelles, and Mauritius—lie off the east coast of Africa. These islands lie between Africa and South Asia. Both regions have had a great influence on these islands' cultural development. People of these islands trace their ancestry to Banti, Asia, Arab, and European backgrounds.

Madagascar

The largest of the islands is Madagascar. It was settled at least 2,000 years ago by people from Southeast Asia. These settlers brought with them Asian farming methods and crops.

Along the east coast of Madagascar lies a narrow, wet coastal plain and a steep cliff topped by a flat plateau. On this escarpment can be found a mild climate and rich soil. West from the edge of the escarpment, the island becomes drier as it slopes down to the coast on the Mozambique Channel. This channel separates Madagascar from the African continent.

As a result of the rich soil and mild climate on the escarpment, Madagascar's farmers can raise crops of coffee, vanilla, sugar, and cloves for export. They raise rice, bananas, cassava, and sweet potatoes. However, most farmers raise barely enough food to survive.

Home to Many Animals

When Europeans first discovered the island of Madagascar, it was thinly populated by humans. It was, however, full of giant tortoises. These tortoises were huge (as much as 500 pounds), slow moving, peaceful vegetarians. Today these tortoises are gone from Madagascar. They may still be found in small numbers on one or two of the smaller islands.

Humpback whales swim off the coast of Madagascar, and chameleons (lizards that can change color to match their surroundings) make their homes in the trees. The lemur, an animal related to the monkey, is found only on Madagascar and the nearby Comoros islands.

Comoros

The four mountainous islands of Comoros are located between Madagascar and Tanzania. The official name of the nation is the Federal Islamic Republic of the Comoros.

Although there is a shortage of good farmland here, due to the island's mountains, most Comorans work as farmers. Rice, cassava, bananas, and coconuts are grown as food products. Spices and copra are raised as cash crops.

Chameleons make their homes in the trees of Madagascar.

Madagascar and the nearby Comoros islands are the only places where lemurs are found.

In general, the Comoros are poor and very overpopulated. There are no minerals or natural resources on the islands. Industry has not developed, except for a small fishing fleet that operates along the coast. The people of the Comoros islands must depend on foreign aid to survive.

The people of the Comoros islands follow the Islamic religion. The official languages of the government are French and Arabic.

Mauritius

Mauritius is a volcanic island that lies in the Indian Ocean about 500 miles east of Madagascar. It has miles of golden beaches surrounded by colorful coral reefs.

Though the islands were uninhabited before their discovery in 1598, today Mauritius is densely populated. Mauritius has been controlled by the Dutch, the French, and the English. Its location in the Indian Ocean between Africa and India made it a **strategic** port for

Processing Sugarcane

Sugarcane is a plant that resembles bamboo. The stalks may grow to be two inches in diameter and up to 30 feet high. A good crop of sugarcane resembles a thick jungle.

After the cane is harvested and sent to the mill, it is shredded and crushed. The crushed cane is then milled, or sent through heavy rollers. This process produces a liquid that is very sweet. This liquid is then processed by heating. The remaining liquid is then evaporated. The result is a crystal that we call sugar.

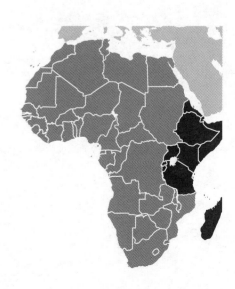

supplying ships. However, the completion of the Suez Canal in 1869 caused the island to become less important.

The Europeans began the raising of sugarcane. The English language and Indian plantation labor were introduced after the English gained control of the island in 1810. Today the economy of Mauritius is controlled by the price of sugar on the world market.

Hindus are the largest religious group. Most other Mauritians are Christians or Muslims. Mauritius has a high literacy rate and high health standards.

Seychelles

Seychelles, made up of more than 90 small islands, is located in the Indian Ocean about 700 miles northeast of Madagascar. Because Seychelles has limited mineral resources, most people earn a living by farming. Their main products are coconuts, vanilla, and cinnamon.

Seychelles has many beautiful coral islands with miles of sandy beaches. With the bonus of year-round sunshine, an important tourist industry has been created. It provides jobs and cash to support the economy and the needs of the people.

In addition, a United States space tracking station on Seychelles employs many local people. This tracking station gives them an important spot where they can look at spacecraft. More important to the people of Seychelles, it brings in American dollars needed to support the local economy. This situation is an excellent example of the way people who live thousands of miles apart can help each other.

LESSON REVIEW

Directions: Answer the following questions in complete sentences.

1. How has geography influenced farming in Madagascar?

2. Why have the people of the Comoros not been able to develop a healthy economy?

3. Why has the development of the tourist industry become important in the Seychelle islands?

4. How have different ethnic groups influenced the people of these islands?

5. What examples of interdependence exist in relation to these islands?

"Dr. Livingstone, I presume?"

Spotlight Story

Europeans Explore Africa

European explorers searched for the source of the Nile River for many years. In 1858 Richard Burton and John Speke discovered Lake Tanganyika in what is now Tanzania. Burton was certain that Lake Tanganyika was the source of the Nile, but Speke was not convinced. Speke trudged on through the jungles and discovered Lake Victoria; he became convinced that it was the source of the Nile.

In a later expedition, Speke returned to Lake Victoria. However, his travels were not without danger. At one point, his party traveled through Buganda (in what is now southern Uganda). He was held prisoner for six months by a great king named Mutesa. Sadly, Speke died with the question of the source of the Nile still not answered.

In March of 1866, Dr. David Livingstone undertook the job of finding the source of the Nile. By this time, there were many theories as to just where the Nile began. Livingstone wandered about Africa for over five years. Many presumed that he was dead, since no one had heard a word from him.

Livingstone was eventually found. A reporter from the *New York Herald*, Henry Morton Stanley, found Livingstone in a small village in November 1871. Upon finding him, Stanley spoke the words, "Dr. Livingstone, I presume?" Livingstone simply responded, "Yes." These words are now part of the culture and heritage of both Great Britain and Africa.

The question about the source of the Nile, however, still went unanswered. Livingstone died in May 1873; he had failed in his attempts to find the source of the Nile. The task then fell to Henry Morton Stanley. In 1874 Stanley set out and finally proved that Lake Victoria was indeed the source of the Nile. Upon his return in 1876, exactly 1,003 days after he had left, Stanley presented proof of his theories and proved that the theories of all the others were wrong.

SPOTLIGHT REVIEW

Answer the following questions.

1. Name four explorers who are associated with the search for the source of the Nile.
2. Identify one source of the Nile that was disproven by Henry Stanley.
3. Name three dangers that explorers faced in their search for the source of the Nile.
4. In what year did Dr. Livingstone first set out to find the source of the Nile?

Chapter 6 Review

In Eastern Africa, wild animals often share the land with human beings; both frequently suffer from the harshness of drought. The droughts in this part of the world are happening more often than in the past. Many tens of thousands of people have been forced from their villages in search of food and water. Countless numbers have died of starvation.

Tanzania is the largest country in Eastern Africa. Mt. Kilimanjaro, the Serengeti Plain, and Olduvai Gorge (where fossils of early humans have been discovered), are all in the country of Tanzania. Uganda is a country that once had a good economy. But the behavior of Idi Amin Dada, at one time president of Uganda, caused Uganda's economy to fall into ruin.

Kenya has few mineral resources. There are many wildlife preserves in Kenya, and people travel there to photograph them. Rwanda and Burundi are both very poor countries. They are crowded, land is scarce, and there is poor soil for growing crops. Ethiopia also has some of the oldest fossils ever discovered. Coffee is a major export, but Ethiopia needs help from other countries to feed all the people. Eritrea was once part of Ethiopia.

Djibouti has few industries and extremely hot temperatures. Somalia is a dry land where few crops can grow. Most of the people in Somalia are nomads. The islands of Madagascar, Comoros, Seychelles, and Mauritius lie off the east coast of Africa. Madagascar is the largest, and many interesting animals live there. Comoros consists of four mountainous islands; they are very crowded. Mauritius is an island that is really the top of an underwater volcano. Seychelles is made up of more than 90 small islands. There are many beautiful coral islands there, and they have a busy tourist industry.

These children are visiting the Afew Giraffe Center in Nairobi, Kenya.

Eastern Africa – Chapter 6

Critical Thinking Skills
Directions: Give some thought to the questions below. Be sure to answer in complete sentences.

1. Explain why David Livingstone went to Africa in the first place.
2. Explain how a language and culture like Swahili might be developed.
3. Why do you think many Falashas have left Ethiopia?
4. Why are cattle so important to the Masai people?
5. How could the people of Somalia have survived for so long without a written language?

For Discussion
1. Explain why the people of Eritrea have revolted in Ethiopia.
2. What items attract tourists to a place like Kenya?
3. For what skills are the Masai famous?
4. Why do the nomads of Somalia wander from place to place?
5. What are some of the things that once made Uganda a wealthy country?

Write It!
Directions: Imagine that you are a member of the United Nations and that it is your job to see to it that the children of East Africa are properly fed. Tomorrow you are to deliver a speech to the General Assembly of the UN. What will you say in your speech?

For You to Do
Directions: Go on a safari. Cut pictures out of magazines, or draw pictures of animals that live in Eastern Africa. Make a collage of this wildlife of Eastern Africa. Then, choose one species of animal and prepare a report for the class. Be sure to include these topics: what it eats, how long it lives, its size, and anything else that you think might be interesting.

NORTH AFRICA

CHAPTER 7

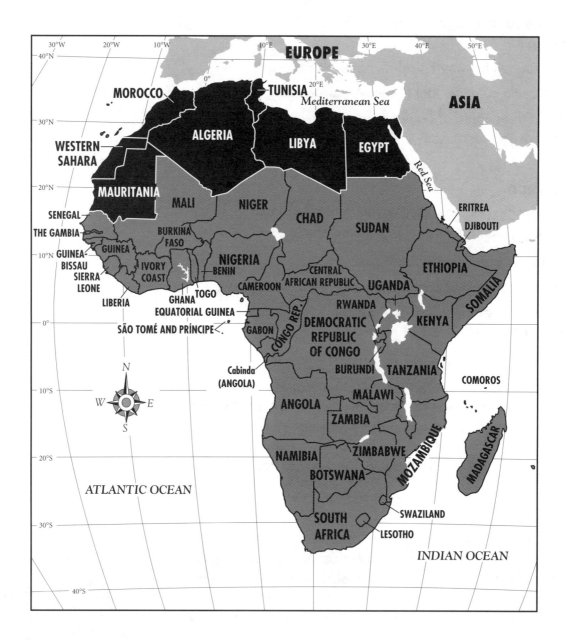

Fast Facts:

- The great pyramids were built entirely by hand, around 2500 B.C.
- Carpet weaving is a vital craft in many parts of Moracco.
- The once-famous fortress of Casbah is located in Algiers, Algeria.
- Egyptians studied mathematics and astronomy as far back as 4000 B.C.
- The Nile River is the longest river in the world, stretching more than 4,000 miles.

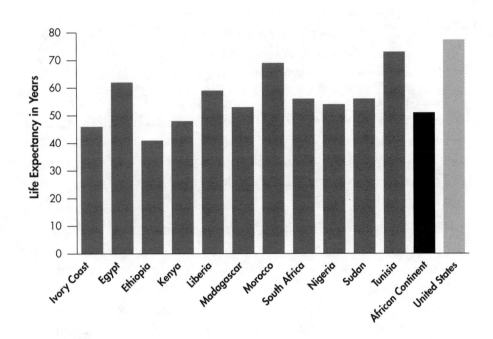

CHART SKILLS

Life Expectancy in Africa

Study the chart above to answer these questions.

1. Which three African countries have the longest life expectancy?

2. Which African country has the shortest life expectancy?

3. Name two countries where the life expectancy is around 50 years.

4. What is the average life expectancy for all of the African countries listed?

5. What is the life expectancy in the United States?

6. What is the expected lifetime for a citizen of the Ivory Coast?

Words to Know

mosque:
a Muslim house of prayer

LESSON 1: Mountains and Deserts

North Africa's Arab countries include Egypt, Libya, Tunisia, Algeria, Morocco, and Western Sahara. Located between Europe and Asia, North Africa has been influenced by many different cultures and traditions. Settlement is concentrated along the shores of the Mediterranean and in areas where irrigation is available.

The Sahara is inhabited by nomadic Bedouins. The word *sahara* comes from the Arab word for "desert." Humans have lived in the Sahara Desert for thousands of years. Ancient oasis towns are located at springs and places where wells can reach water below dry riverbeds. The few roads crossing the Sahara follow old caravan routes from oasis to oasis.

The people who live in North Africa today are mostly Arabs and Berbers. Traditions are important to them, especially religion. These Muslims strictly follow the teachings of their holy book, called the *Koran*. Muslims pray in a **mosque**, a distinctive type of building seen very often in North African cities. The language of the people is Arabic. Important Arab civilizations have existed for thousands of years.

The Berber people are slightly more difficult to describe. Historians know that the Berbers have lived throughout North Africa for thousands of years. However, no one is sure of their origins. The Berbers maintain their own religious beliefs and their own language.

Travelers going from east to west across North Africa encounter some of the most contrasting types of land in all the world. North Africans are blessed with hundreds of miles of scenic Mediterranean and Atlantic coastlines. The majestic, fertile Nile River Valley and the high, snowcapped Atlas Mountains are also found in this region. In sharp contrast to these beautiful landscapes is the forbidding vastness of the Sahara.

LESSON REVIEW

Directions: Answer the following questions in complete sentences.

1. Describe some different geographical features of North Africa.

2. What is the name of a Muslim house of prayer?

3. What is the name of the Muslim holy book?

4. Where are most of the cities of North Africa located?

5. What does the word *sahara* mean?

LESSON 2: Egypt—An Ancient Civilization

From the Red Sea, across Egypt just a short distance, one can see the Nile River. It's the longest river in the world. Without the Nile River and an oasis here and there, very few people would live in this area because it is mainly desert. The Nile provides water, fertile crop lands, and jobs for millions of people. Cities were being built in this valley over five thousand years ago.

As far back as 4000 B.C., the Egyptians irrigated their farms, studied astronomy and mathematics, and made fine pottery. By 3000 B.C., these civilized people were hard at work building the great pyramids.

The Great Sphinx and the ancient pyramids are near Cairo, the capital of Egypt.

Ancient Pyramids

The great pyramids were actually tombs built for the pharaohs, the rulers of ancient Egypt. These huge buildings, some as long as two city blocks, were built entirely by hand. In 2500 B.C., the Egyptians did not have the machines that we have today. For that reason, it probably took many people a very long time to build the pyramids.

The Fellahin

More than half of the people in Egypt today make their living as farmers. However, only about 4 percent of the land is suitable for farming. This land is located primarily in the Nile Valley. It is farmed by peasant farmers called fellahin. Most of Egypt's fellahin live in villages close to their farmland.

Words to Know

sphinx:
an ancient Egyptian construction, built to look like part man and part lion

Egyptian Cities

In contrast, Egypt has two very large cities, Alexandria and Cairo. Alexandria serves as Egypt's major seaport and is located on the Mediterranean Sea. From this point, ships pass through the Suez Canal that connects the Mediterranean and the Red Sea.

Cairo is the capital of Egypt and the largest city in all of Africa. More than seven million people live in this city. From Cairo, it is only a few miles to the ancient pyramids and the Great **Sphinx**. Although some parts of Cairo are thousands of years old, other parts are new. Modern Cairo looks very much like any large city in the United States.

LESSON REVIEW

Directions: Number your paper from 1 to 5. Then answer the following questions.

1. List three things that the Nile River provides to the people of Egypt.

2. Why were the pyramids built?

3. What are peasant farmers in the Nile Valley called?

4. What is the name of the largest city in Africa?

5. How much of the land in Egypt can be used for farming?

LESSON 3: Libya and Tunisia

To the west of Egypt is the country of Libya. This nation is much larger than Egypt, but only about five million people live in the entire country. This is because most of Libya is in the Sahara.

No people can live in the Sahara unless they live near an oasis. An oasis is a spot in the desert where there is water and fertile soil. Oases depend upon seasonal rivers or deep wells for water. Some oases are found at the foot of a mountain and get their water from springs.

Because so much of Libya is desert, little farming takes place. The farmers in Libya grow barley, wheat, citrus fruits, olives, dates, and almonds. Most of the farms in Libya are found near the Mediterranean Sea. However, even near the Mediterranean rain is undependable, and very often Libya must import food.

The discovery of oil has helped to modernize Libyan cities like Tripoli and Benghazi. If one compares Cairo and Alexandria in Egypt to Tripoli and Benghazi in Libya, the latter two cities are smaller and newer. The skyline of Benghazi is dominated by a mix of office buildings, hotels, and mosques.

Tunisia

Northwest of Libya is Tunisia, a small country on the Mediterranean coast. Most of Tunisia's nine million people live near the coast. The capital of Tunisia is Tunis.

Workers must climb tall date palms to pick the dates.

Words to Know

dune:
a hill or ridge of sand

indigenous:
occurring naturally in an area; native

Most farms are located in the northern part of the country. Tunisian farmers grow wheat, olives, and grapes. However, rain in this part of the world can be scarce. In years of drought, the government must provide food and jobs, or many people will starve.

Many Tunisians make a living fishing. The Mediterranean Sea is like their farm. They harvest tuna, shrimp, sardines, and lobsters.

The beautiful coastline of Tunisia faces Europe, which is only 86 miles away. For over 2,500 years, Europeans have come to Tunisia to travel and to trade. Because of this exchange, Tunisia is much like a typical European country.

Tunis, the capital of Tunisia, stands where Carthage used to be.

Hannibal's March across the Alps

Many years ago, there was a city in Tunisia named Carthage. The people of Carthage were at war with the Romans. That's when one of history's most famous generals, Hannibal, of Carthage, mounted an attack against Rome. Hannibal's army, which used elephants to carry equipment, came within 30 miles of Rome before they stopped. Many stories have been written about General Hannibal's great march across the Alps.

LESSON REVIEW

**Directions: Number your paper from 1 to 5.
Write *true* or *false* to describe each statement.**

1. Little farming is done in Libya.

2. Libya sits atop great oil fields.

3. Oases are fed by water from the ocean.

4. Libya is smaller in size than Egypt.

5. Tunisia has frequent floods.

LESSON 4: Algeria and Mauritania

Algeria, like Tunisia, is very close to Europe. Algeria has, at different times, been ruled by Spain, Turkey, and France. Today, many Algerians still speak French. Algeria's population clusters around the northern part of the country. Its farmers grow the typical North African crops of olives, citrus fruits, and grapes. The Saharan part of Algeria is largely unpopulated except near oases. The people there are mostly Berbers or Arabs.

Algiers is the capital city of Algeria. In Algiers, tourists often visit the Casbah, once a famous fortress, now an exciting, crowded mix of shops and housing.

Some Muslim women, such as this woman from Algiers, wear traditional dress.

Mauritania

From the western tip of Algeria, one can move south into Mauritania. Much of this country lies in the Sahara, where there is nothing but endless stretches of sand. The desert continues for mile after mile, broken only by a **dune** or a few barren rocks.

In the south of Mauritania live the Fulani and the Tukulor. The Fulani raise cattle, and the Tukulor make a living by farming or fishing.

The people who live in the northern part of Mauritania are called Moors. The French call them Maures and named the country for them. These people are a mixture of Arabs, Berbers, and **indigenous** Africans.

The Sahara seems to have been made for the Mauritanians. They are outstanding herdsmen and raise sheep, camels, and goats.

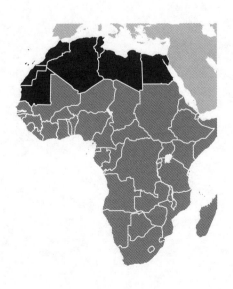

The Mauritanians are nomads, which means that they move from place to place. They travel frequently so that their herds will have enough water to drink. Living in the desert for many generations has made the Moors the masters of the Sahara.

There are no major cities in Mauritania because of the way the Moors live their lives. Nomads have little use for a city. Still, Mauritania has a capital city called Nouakchott.

LESSON REVIEW

Directions: Number your paper from 1 to 5. Write one word to complete each sentence

1. The Sahara is made of nothing but _____.

2. Mauritania is to the _____ of Algeria.

3. Mauritania is named for the people who live there called _____.

4. Nouakchott is the capital city of _____.

5. The Tukulor live by farming and _____.

LESSON 5: Visiting Morocco

The last countries in North Africa are Morocco and Western Sahara. Western Sahara is a very small country that has been taken over by Morocco. Morocco is located at the extreme northwest corner of Africa. The high, rugged Atlas Mountains cover much of Morocco. Because of their geographic location, Moroccans have long been familiar with both European and American customs.

On our visit to Morocco, we will stay with the Bakkali family. They will greet us at Casablanca's modern international airport. This is not surprising, since the Moroccans like to welcome visitors and treat them well.

The nomads of North Africa travel the Sahara, moving from one water source to another.

Family Life

The Bakkali family is a typical Moroccan family. Malik Bakkali is a 13-year-old boy. His sister, Fatima, is two years older; and his other sister, Aisha, is 11. Mrs. Bakkali dresses traditionally and wears a *jellaba*. This is a long, flowing cotton robe that covers Mrs. Bakkali from her neck to her ankles. She also wears a veil to cover her face. Fatima has chosen to be a more modern young woman. Her dress is much like what you might see in your own neighborhood. Mr. Bakkali works in a factory in Casablanca. His clothing is also similar to what Europeans or Americans would wear.

In Morocco children between the ages of 7 and 13 must attend school. One-third of all Moroccans continue in school past the age of 13. All three children attend day school. They study the same subjects that students in the United States do, except they learn Arabic as a first language. Almost all school-aged children also learn French.

Words to Know

Ramadan:
the Muslim holy month

Shopping in Morocco

Before going to the Bakkalis' house, we stop at the *souk*, or marketplace. The market in Casablanca is an open market with rows and rows of stalls. In some ways, the souks are like huge malls. Shoppers in the souk can buy almost anything that they need. Vendors sell fruit, fresh vegetables, eggs, candy, and even televisions! There are doctors in the markets, as well as snake charmers and restaurants.

As we wander through the souk, we come to a stall full of colorful carpets. They are handmade of wool and dyed in a pattern. Each family has its own unique design. Nearby, people work with leather and gold. Toward the outer edge of the souk, we can even buy a camel if we wish!

Mountain Villages

While in Morocco, we plan to visit a nearby mountain village. Jbila is in the foothills of the Atlas Mountains. Life in Jbila is very different from life in the large city of Casablanca. The people are all farmers. There are only 20 houses in the entire village.

Village farms are very small—less than three acres. Wheat, barley, and vegetables are usually grown there. Some livestock—such as goats, chickens, and perhaps a cow—can be found on a village farm. The entire family works on the farm.

People from the village travel to a nearby souk to sell their crops. That is the way they get dirhams (their money) to buy supplies. The village people might have to walk six or eight hours to get to the souk. Many village families make things themselves instead of buying them.

Evening Entertainment

When we return to Casablanca, we are going to a fantasia. The fantasia is a display of the fine horse riding skills of the Arabs and Berbers.

As we watch, ten men in white robes and turbans race their horses toward the spectators. The men carry beautiful weapons—shiny guns and jeweled daggers. At the last second, they stop only a few feet away from where we stand. The riders fire their guns in the sky. The crowd cheers as another group of riders ready their horses.

Religion Is Very Important

The Bakkalis explained that in their religion they pray five times a day. A caller, known as a muezzin, summons them to prayer from the top of the mosque's minaret, or tower. Devoted Muslims stop whatever they are doing, get out their prayer mats, and face Mecca. Mecca is the holy city of the Islamic faith. It is located in Saudi Arabia.

An important observance in the Islam religion is **Ramadan**. This holy month is the ninth month of the Islamic calendar. Each day during Ramadan, adult Muslims fast, or go without food and water, from dawn to sunset.

LESSON REVIEW

Directions: Number your paper from 1 to 5. Then answer the following questions.

1. What two languages do Moroccan children learn in school?

2. What is the Arabic word for marketplace?

3. What is the unit of money used in Morocco?

4. What is the name of the person who calls Muslims to prayer?

5. What is the name of the Muslim holy month?

Spotlight Story
An Evening with the Bakkalis

Before entering the Bakkalis' house, we take off our shoes. Only *babouches*, or slippers, can be worn inside a Moroccan house. Their house is old and small. There is a kitchen, three rooms upstairs, and a storage room. Two of the upstairs rooms are bedrooms, and the third is used as a room for family gatherings. Like most Moroccans, the Bakkalis have a garden in the rear of the house.

Mrs. Bakkali and Fatima are preparing the evening meal. They are making the *diffa*, a traditional meal of welcome for visitors to a Moroccan home. As we wait for dinner to be served, Aisha settles in front of the television. In Morocco television sets are very expensive, and many families do not own one. Most television shows in Morocco are shown in Arabic or French. Because Morocco is so close to Spain, Moroccan television also shows Spanish stations.

Malik goes off to the soccer field while dinner is being prepared. He loves many sports such as basketball, volleyball, and field hockey. Swimming, track and field, gymnastics, and boxing are other popular sports in Morocco, but Malik doesn't have time to participate in every sport.

Finally, the evening meal is ready. Everyone sits around a low table. Mr. Bakkali says "*Bismillah*," which means "in the name of God." Then a bowl is passed around for everyone to wash his or her hands.

Moroccans do not use forks. They eat with their right hand. It is not considered bad manners as long as your right hand is clean. The left hand is used for other tasks and is not put in the food dish.

Mrs. Bakkali begins the meal with *tajine*, a stew made from meat—usually chicken, pigeon, or beef. The stew is thick so that it can be eaten with the fingers. Next comes *mechoui*, or roast mutton. Mutton is the meat from a sheep. Then comes *couscous*, a boiled grain with spices or sweetening. Water is on the table, but no one takes a drink while eating.

Dessert consists of pastries and a bowl of delicious fresh oranges. Adults drink mint tea with dessert. The children drink orange juice or milk made from crushed almonds. The Muslim religion forbids the drinking of alcohol.

After dinner Mr. Bakkali plays a flute, and Malik plays a *rebab*, the Moroccan fiddle. The two play classical Moroccan music called Andalusian.

SPOTLIGHT REVIEW

Write *same* if what is written is done the same way in the United States. Write *different* if it is done differently.

1. Forks are not used.
2. The large meal of the day is eaten in the evening.
3. Most television shows are in French.
4. Dessert is a sweet or a piece of fruit.
5. Milk comes from crushed almonds.

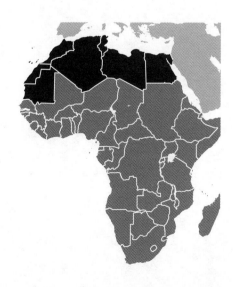

Chapter 7 Review

The area called North Africa is very different from the other regions of Africa. There civilizations have flourished for thousands of years. The Egyptians are perhaps the oldest organized civilization in the world. Egypt is home to the great pyramids. The Nile River flows through Egypt, providing much-needed water. More than half of the people in Egypt make their living as farmers.

North Africa has had contact with its European neighbors for centuries. Many of the features of North Africa have been influenced by Europeans. Some of the people in North Africa are of Arabic or Berber ancestry. The North African countries can be divided into two regions. In or near the hot Sahara, nothing lives or grows. However, near the coast and along the Nile River, cities grow and people thrive. For this reason, the North African countries are not as poor as many of their southern neighbors.

Most of Libya is in the Sahara, so little farming takes place there. Many people in Tunisia make a living fishing in the Mediterranean. Tunisia is much like a typical European country.

Algeria is very close to Europe. It has been ruled by Spain, Turkey, and France. Much of Mauritania is in the Sahara, and the people there are nomads. There are no major cities in Mauritania.

The Moors use camels to travel in the desert because camels can go without water for a long time.

Critical Thinking Skills

Directions: Give some thought to the questions below. Be sure to answer in complete sentences.

1. Why are the populations of Tunisia, Algeria, and Libya clustered around the coastline?

2. How has the discovery of oil in Libya changed the way Libyans live?

3. Why is the varied wildlife of Equatorial and Eastern Africa not found in North Africa?

4. What industries can be carried on in coastal cities that may not be carried on farther inland?

For Discussion

1. In what ways would North Africa be different without the Nile River?

2. How do the Arabs of North Africa differ from most of the people who live in the rest of Africa?

3. Which seems to be a bigger influence on North Africa, the Nile River or the Sahara? Why?

4. Lesson 3 of this chapter stated that Tunisia is like a typical European country. What do you think this means?

5. How are the mountain villages of Morocco similar to its cities? How are they different?

Write It!

Imagine being a nomad in North Africa. What things would you do and what would you want to have with you before you entered the desert?

For You to Do

Directions: Reread the Spotlight Story in this chapter. Write a report of about the same length. Describe the day-to-day customs in your house. Explain to a Moroccan reader how your evening meal is eaten. Describe what members of your family are doing before and after the meal.

adobe (ə dō´ bē) a building material made of sun-dried and sun-baked earth mixed with straw

animism (an´ ə miz əm) the belief that spirits occupy all objects, both living and nonliving

anthropologist (an thrə pol´ ə jist) a person who studies the science of humankind and compares human cultures

apartheid (ə pärt´ hīt) a system of race relations, officially used in South Africa 1948-94, whereby the races were separated in power and status, with whites dominating blacks

asbestos (as bes´ təs) mineral that does not burn or conduct heat

bauxite (bȯk´ sīt) a mineral ore used in making aluminum

bronze (bronz) a mixture of copper and another element, usually tin

cacao (kə kā´ ō) the seeds from which cocoa and chocolate are made

calabash (kal´ ə bash) a type of gourd

cash crop (kash krop) a crop that is raised for sale and export rather than for one's own use

cassava (kə sä´ və) a tropical plant with starchy roots; tapioca is made from cassava root

caste (kast) class or group of people

Christianity (kris chē an´ ə tē) the religion derived from Jesus Christ and based on the Old Testament and New Testament of the Bible as sacred scripture

civil war (siv´ əl wôr) a war between groups of people of a single area or country

civilian (sə vil´ yən) a person who is not in the armed services or military

coastal plain (kō´ stl plān) a flat, sea-level area usually near an ocean

cobalt (kōl´ bȯlt) a hard, metallic element used in combining metals

colony (kä´ lə nē) a group of people living in a territory but keeping ties with the parent nation

copra (kō´ prə) the dried meat of coconuts; coconut oil comes from copra

coup d'etat (kü dā tä´) sudden overthrow of a government

delta (del´ tə) the land at the mouth of a river

developing country (di vel´ ə ping kən´ trē) countries improving in technology and quality of living after becoming self-governing

GLOSSARY

dialect (dī´ ə lekt) a particular form of a language

dictator (dik´ tā tər) a ruler who uses absolute authority or power that must be obeyed

discriminate (dis krim´ ə nāt) to treat one person or group of people better than another; prejudicial outlook, action, or treatment

dominate (dom´ ə nāt) to control by strength or power

dowry (dou´ rē) money or property given by a man to or for his bride; in some cultures, it is the money or goods that a woman brings to her husband in marriage

dune (dün) a hill or ridge of sand

dynasty (dī´ nə stē) a group or family that rules from one generation to the next

ebony (eb´ ə nē) a very hard black wood

economic (ek ə nom´ ik) having to do with earning a living and producing goods and services

economy (ikon´ ə mē) the way in which a group or nation provides for the needs and desires of its people

escarpment (e skärp´ mənt) sharp, steep cliffs

ethnic (eth´ nik) a group of people who share a common culture and history

eucalyptus (yü kə lip´ təs) an evergreen tree with useful wood, gums, resins, and oils

exotic (eg zot´ ik) wildly different or unusual to the beholder

fossil (fos´ əl) traces of earlier life forms preserved in rock

goldsmith (gōld´ smith) a person who crafts gold

guerrilla (gə ril´ ə) people who attack an enemy suddenly, who are not members of a regular army

gum arabic (gum ar´ ə bik) a substance from acacia trees, used to make candy and medicine

hardwood (härd´ wùd) a tree that does not produce its seeds in cones

heritage (her´ ə tij) traditions inherited or passed down from one generation to another

a	hat	e	let	ī	ice	ô	order	ù	put	sh	she	ə	a in about
ā	age	ē	equal	o	hot	oi	oil	ü	rule	th	thin		e in taken
ä	far	ėr	term	ō	open	ou	out	ch	child	ᴛʜ	then		i in pencil
â	care	i	it	ȯ	saw	u	cup	ng	long	zh	measure		o in lemon
													u in circus

GLOSSARY

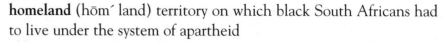

homeland (hōm´ land) territory on which black South Africans had to live under the system of apartheid

illiterate (i lit´ ər it) having little or no education; unable to read or write

indigenous (in dij´ ə nəs) occurring naturally in an area; native

inhospitable (in ho spit´ ə bəl) not friendly or receptive; providing no shelter or sustenance

intermarriage (in tər mar´ ij) marriage of persons of different ethnic or religious groups

invincible (in vin´ sə bəl) incapable of being conquered

Islam (is´ ləm) a world religion stating the belief that Allah is the only god and that Muhammad is his prophet

javelin (jav´ lən) a light spear thrown by hand

landform (land´ fôrm) a physical feature of the earth's surface, such as plains, plateaus, hills or mountains

landlocked (land´ lokt) a country or place that is surrounded by land and that has no access to a sea or ocean

mahogany (mə hog´ ə nē) a dark tropical tree, usually yellowish to reddish brown

manganese (mang´ gə nēz) hard, brittle, grayish metallic element used to make steel, in paints, dyes, etc.

mangrove (man´ grōv) tropical trees or shrubs with many roots that look like extra trunks and form dense masses

millet (mil´ it) any of several cereal grasses, grown for food or hay

mosque (mosk) a Muslim house of prayer

Muslim (muz´ ləm) a person who follows the religion of Islam

nomad (nō´ mad) a person whose home moves from one place to another

palm (päm) tall trees with tall trunk and branches, with large leaves at the top; palm kernels are used to make food, oil and starch, and palm fiber is used to make rope

phosphate (fos´ fāt) a salt of phosphoric acid used in bread or fertilizer

piassava (pē ə sä´ və) a palm tree whose fibers are used to make brooms

pollute (pə lüt´) to make dirty

potential (pə ten´ shəl) possibility of future development and improvement

GLOSSARY

preserve (pri zėrv´) a place where wild animals roam freely and are protected by law from hunters

protectorate (prə tek´ tər it) a weak country under the protection and partial control of a strong country

rain forest (rān fôr´ ist) a thick tropical forest

Ramadan (räm ə dän´) the Muslim holy month

safari (sə fär´ ē) an expedition, usually for hunting or photographing wildlife

sanction (sangk´ shən) economic measure used to force a country to change its behavior or laws

savanna (sə van´ ə) a tropical grassland with scattered trees

Semite (sem´ īt) a person from a Middle Eastern or Arab country

shaman (shä´ mən) a person believed to have close contact with the spirit world; medicine man

silt (silt) dirt or sediment that is washed into and carried by rivers

sisal (sī´ səl) a strong white fiber used for making rope or twine

sorghum (sôr´ gəm) a tall grass resembling corn; the grain is used for food, the stems and leaves as animal fodder, and the stalks are used as thatching for houses

sphinx (sfingks) an ancient Egyptian construction, built to look like part man and part lion

strategic (strə tē´ jik) necessary or important to carry out a plan

sub-Saharan (sub sə hâr´ ən) describes the part of Africa south of the Sahara

subsistence (səb sis´ təns) producing a minimum return and a level of bare existence

synthetic (sin the´ tik) not real; artificial

taboo (tə bü´) forbidden by custom or by tradition

tactic (tak´ tik) system or planned procedure

terra-cotta (ter´ ə kot´ ə) a baked clay used in pottery

topography (tə pog´ rə fē) the surface features of the land

a	hat	e	let	ī	ice	ô	order	ủ	put	sh	she		a	in about
ā	age	ē	equal	o	hot	oi	oil	ü	rule	th	thin	ə	e	in taken
ä	far	ėr	term	ō	open	ou	out	ch	child	ᵺ	then		i	in pencil
â	care	i	it	ȯ	saw	u	cup	ng	long	zh	measure		o	in lemon
													u	in circus

GLOSSARY

township (toun´ ship) a residential area established to house black South Africans who are kept from having homes in urban areas

tradition (trə dish´ ən) a custom, idea, or belief handed down from one person to the next

tributary (trib´ yə ter ē) a branch of a river

tsetse fly (tset´ sē flī) a type of fly that carries and spreads sleeping sickness

uranium (yù rā´ nē əm) a radioactive element

urban (ėr´ bən) relating to a city

INDEX